PSYCHEDELIC PSYCHOTHERAPY

A User-friendly Guide for
Psychedelic Drug-assisted Psychotherapy

PSYCHEDELIC PSYCHOTHERAPY

A User-friendly Guide for Psychedelic Drug-assisted Psychotherapy

by R. Coleman

Printed in the United States of America

For information contact:
TRANSFORM PRESS
PO BOX 11552
BERKELEY, CA 94712

www.transformpress.com

First Edition
ISBN-10: 0-9630096-5-6
ISBN-13: 978-0-9630096-5-4

Cover Design by Mitchell Walker

PSYCHEDELIC PSYCHOTHERAPY

INTRODUCTION

The use of psychedelics for healing is a practice thousands of years old, and is well-documented in indigenous cultures all over the world. Today, psychedelic drugs are proving to be extraordinary catalysts that accelerate healing and transcend the limitations of mainstream psychotherapy.

Psychedelic drugs are commonly associated with young people getting high in stimulating, hedonistic, social environments like music festivals. Although most people today know of psychedelics only as recreational drugs, their earliest recorded uses were religious and therapeutic. In the 1950s and '60s, hundreds of psychotherapy sessions were conducted using LSD and other substances. This work went underground but did not end when psychedelics were made illegal. Courageous therapists and guides willing to risk working outside the law found that psychedelics allowed them to help people who had not responded to conventional treatment.

This manual is intended to be a resource for those using psychedelic drugs for psychological healing in controlled, therapeutic settings that promote focused introspection. This guide is dedicated to suffering individuals who seek to be truly free from the debilitating effects of childhood trauma, and to those who wish to help them.

The information contained herein was learned during three decades of the author's personal healing and professional experience facilitating thousands of psychedelic therapy sessions.

This is by no means THE definitive guide to all the possible ways psychedelics can be used for healing. There are many other known and yet to be discovered ways that psychedelics can facilitate psychological healing, personal growth, and spiritual awakening.

Psychedelics are powerful but potentially dangerous tools to access the human psyche. Use these drugs with great caution. Psychedelic therapy requires courage and determination to face one's deepest fears. The process can be challenging and painful--it should not be undertaken alone. Psychedelic therapy can be profoundly transformational, when used in a careful and informed manner.

Note: In this guide, psychedelic sessions are referred to as "journeys." Time spent in an altered state is referred to as "journeyspace." All journey stories and excerpts are from actual sessions.

The Author's Story

In my early twenties, I was disturbed by the suffering and madness in the world. I embarked on a quest to find the meaning and purpose of life. My search led me to a guide who introduced me to psychedelics. During my sessions, I had transcendent, mystical experiences that expanded my worldview beyond the confines of my five senses. I experienced my life as a brief moment in infinite time and space. I awakened from the trance of limiting beliefs and mundane, consensus reality. I felt connected to God, my soul, and the sacredness of all living things. My spiritual life soared, but serious health, sexual, and relationship issues persisted. I still suffered from chronic fatigue, depression, and bleeding ulcers in my colon.

I tried treating my symptoms with conventional and alternative medicine. This approach produced some relief, but did not get to the root cause. I searched for psychosomatic origins. Psychotherapy was expensive and frustratingly slow.

I felt like I was rearranging deck chairs on a capsizing Titanic. I was sinking. I was suicidal.

One day, I met a therapist who recommended using MDMA to get "unstuck." From the very first session, I began making amazing breakthroughs. The split between my mind and body began to dissolve. Being present in my body became an experience, not a concept. My heart opened. I could access blocked emotions as never before. As I continued psychedelic therapy, I discovered and worked through trauma of childhood neglect and abuse. Hidden sources of my chronic illness, anxiety, and depression were revealed. My colitis healed, my depression vanished, and my health improved. As my sexual and relationship issues healed, I was able to manifest the healthy, happy marriage I enjoy today.

I spent years in cognitive and Reichian therapy before I discovered psychedelic-assisted psychotherapy. I meditated, practiced yoga, got

Rolfed and rebirthed. All these were helpful, but were only able to take me so far. I believe that without the help of psychedelics I would never have healed. Psychedelic therapy saved my life.

1. PSYCHEDELICS AND HEALING

Psychedelic work is distinct from any other healing modality currently available. Psychiatric medication is designed to extinguish or alleviate symptoms. Psychotherapy and Psychoanalysis aim at finding solutions through cognitive and behavioral modification or through construction of a long-term healing relationship between therapist and client. Even when augmented by clinical hypnosis, dreamwork, energy psychology, and other excellent techniques, the healing of deeply entrenched defense patterns arising from profound early trauma, if successful at all, takes many years in talk-based therapies. Bodywork, breathwork, and other body-centered healing modalities may bypass the body-mind defenses, but they cannot tap as deeply into our innate mechanisms for healing as do properly used psychedelics.

Psychedelics permit the innate intelligence of the body, developed during five million years of evolution, to step in and unleash natural healing from the inside. They allow healing at the root cause of our ailment, be it physical, emotional, cognitive, spiritual, or a combination of these. They work in the places the intellect is afraid, or unable, to go. Psychedelics quickly zero in on the blocks, constrictions, dysfunctions, and mental distortions that accumulate over a lifetime. Psychedelics permit an individual to access unconscious and highly defended memories that are accessible through other modalities only after many years of work, and sometimes not even then. They cut through denial and provide a safe container for the release of trauma. They provide the clarity and openness that lead to integration, making it possible for people to reclaim their whole, fully-functional selves and realize their highest potential.

These pages offer the collective experience, knowledge, thoughts, and observations of practitioners and subjects who have used psychedelics for healing. The field is new, the work experimental and groundbreaking. What works for one person may be of little or no help to others. No doubt, scores of additional psychedelic healing techniques will emerge as this work continues to gain acceptance. The information provided here is offered as a kind of rough roadmap--an early travel guide to an as yet sparsely traveled land.

2. HOW PSYCHEDELIC THERAPY HEALS TRAUMA

Evolution has equipped humans with a variety of mechanisms to encourage survival, even in the face of major traumatic injury. Important among these survival mechanisms is dissociation. "Dissociation" means that trauma is not being felt, experienced, absorbed, or assimilated by the person to whom it is happening. A traumatic injury can be so emotionally overwhelming that the stress could kill a person or bring on a psychotic breakdown. But if some or all awareness of the trauma can be set aside, or experienced as something else while it is happening, the survivor may be able to withstand the initial impact. Later, when they have reached safety and become stronger, they can feel the trauma and let it go.

For example, imagine you are driving up a winding mountain road at night. Suddenly, an oncoming eighteen-wheeler careens across the center meridian, speeding right towards you! You panic, swerve, and narrowly escape a head-on collision. Your heart races and your body shakes, but you must keep driving another eighty miles to reach a place where you can pull over and calm down. To carry on, you have to override your fear and your body's reactions by suppressing your breath, tensing your muscles, and blocking your thoughts of the incident until you get to the place where you can safely "fall apart" and recover. Something like that happens in response to any highly threatening incident when there is no safe way to process the pain and emotion out of the nervous system.

Infants and children are especially prone to dissociate in threatening situations. They have far fewer resources than adults to help them deal with trauma. They don't have strong, developed bodies, fighting skills, strategic thinking, a secure sense of self, or a calming belief system. Their immature nervous systems cannot process all the physical and emotional distress generated by traumatic events or circumstances.

When traumatic events happen to children today, they respond the same way our ancestors responded when threatened by a saber-toothed tiger. They dissociate from the overwhelming terror, setting it aside to be felt and released later. They are able to postpone the full, head-on experience until sufficient resources are available (i.e., Mom and safety) to feel and gradually release feelings they were unable to process at the time of traumatic injury or life-threatening danger.

Sadly, for many infants and children, Mom doesn't come--or she doesn't represent safety and support. Perhaps she died in an auto accident where the child is left alive, frozen with terror, and alone. Perhaps she is drunk or high, and her long absence or crazy behavior is the source of the child's terror. Perhaps the child never finds a place that feels safe until much later in life. The mechanism that allows feelings from traumatic experiences to be postponed permits such a child to survive and function into adulthood even though the trauma remains frozen within their muscles, nerves, brain, and psyche as if it were still happening. This frozen trauma lies at the root of many persistent psychological problems and psychosomatic medical disorders.

Over time, inner walls that were built to keep trauma at bay harden and solidify. We become the walking wounded, numb and unremembering, but bleeding inside. Much of our energy is required to keep the walls between our conscious existence and the wounded part of ourselves intact. Our "normal" or even "happy" childhood is a fiction our minds invent that, if repeated over and over, 24 hours a day, becomes almost true. Psychedelics act like the little boy in the story, "The Emperor's New Clothes." They give us an objective look from outside our ordinary thinking, which lays bare the lies we tell ourselves, the things we run from, and the parts of ourselves we don't want to look at. In the safe and sympathetic presence of our sitter, it is liberating to see these truths. Finally we can begin releasing the trauma. Soon we see the ways our repressed early trauma is creating the emotional and physical dysfunction in our current lives. More and more we discern the walls built on fiction, and allow them to dissolve in the face of truth. As we do so, we can achieve a more grounded, honest, fluid, and happy participation in our own lives.

As our minds release the trauma, so do our bodies. Clenched muscles loosen, allowing us to feel more bodily pleasure. Energy previously used to block off pain is now free to revitalize the body as a vehicle for living.

Psychedelic drugs can be used to explore the depths of the psyche like submarines are used to explore the depths of the ocean. Effective transformational therapy requires that we dive into the unconscious thoughts and emotions that lie deeply submerged beneath the surface of our ordinary awareness. Because the unconscious psyche is seldom accessible to our normal, everyday waking consciousness, we need to alter our consciousness to access this realm experientially. Therapists use dreams and altered state-inducing techniques such as free association, hypnosis, special breathing and body work to access the unconscious. Rarely can these non-drug modalities reach the unconscious as deeply, directly and profoundly as do psychedelic drugs used in controlled therapeutic settings. Without the help of these drugs, the adventure of self-exploration may be limited to relatively shallow waters.

Deep emotional healing can be an excruciatingly slow process, typically requiring years of expensive, weekly psychotherapy sessions that many suffering people can't afford. People who begin serious healing in midlife might not want to spend years in therapy that yields limited results. Recovery from trauma is a challenging odyssey. To complete the journey, travelers must access repressed memories and associated emotions which may be shrouded in amnesia. Traumatic memories often lack verbal narrative or context; rather, they are stored and encoded in the form of bodily sensations, feelings, and images. These memories and emotions are encased in thick walls of muscular armoring, denial, and fear. Most therapies laboriously scratch at the surface of these walls. Psychedelic drugs miraculously melt them. Psychedelics are seldom a quick fix, but they have proven to be a near-miraculous tool for enhancing and accelerating the deepest alchemy of the psyche.

Using psychedelics to heal trauma is not for everyone. It's not recommended for those living with psychotic and borderline disorders. But for adventurous, motivated souls who are resistant to, or impatient with, mainstream therapies, these medicines are cutting-edge tools to access the inner worlds of body, mind, and spirit.

3. LAYERS OF THE PSYCHEDELIC HEALING PROCESS

If you are drawn to explore psychedelic therapy, you are probably motivated by pain and frustration. You may suffer from chronic depression or anxiety. You might struggle with addictions. You may be unhappy with your life, and unsuccessful in your career or relationships. Perhaps you tried many forms of self-help, medications, and mainstream therapies but have been disappointed with the results. Psychedelics may be the missing tool that gets you unstuck.

Psychedelic therapy is an exciting, profound experiential voyage into the vast, mysterious, inner realm of the body and psyche. Your psychedelic therapy sessions may be nothing like you expected, read about, or imagined. Your experiences will be unique to you, but there are elements that are common.

Awareness

You can't fix something you don't know is broken. Therefore, the first step towards healing is to become aware of where you are broken. Without self-awareness you sleepwalk through life, plagued by inexplicable symptoms, bumping into unseen roadblocks, blindly repeating self-sabotaging behaviors and life scripts. The consciousness-expanding properties of psychedelics expose thoughts, feelings, sensations, and phenomena that are normally hidden from your conscious awareness. Once this unconscious material is brought to light, you can begin the healing process.

Early in your explorations you may become keenly aware of self-defeating patterns of behavior. You may also see the social masks and roles you've played to avoid pain and gain acceptance. You'll discover denied, repressed parts of yourself that are vulnerable, soft, innocent, pure, powerful, wise, luminous, primal, dark, deceitful, afraid, angry, brokenhearted, etc. As you embrace or heal these parts, you will get better at creating a satisfying life. You will also be more comfortable being genuine, honest, and compassionate with yourself and others.

You may become conscious of psychological defenses such as projection and denial as you catch yourself using them. Psychological concepts you may have understood intellectually now become tangible experience.

You may encounter visions like demons, deities, and mythological archetypes. These visions often symbolize parts of yourself, significant others, spiritual phenomena, or emerging patterns that may be explored, integrated, or healed.

You may experience profound inner peace, transcendental bliss, and other states of consciousness beyond what you have known. You may experience being vibrantly alive, spontaneous, and open-hearted. You may be less guarded, more relaxed, and more in touch with emotions than you can remember. As these states become imprinted and integrated into consciousness, you will be more able to access them without drugs.

You may experience yourself as pure consciousness beyond your mind and body. You may discover your Higher Self in the form of deep inner wisdom, intuition, spirit guides, animal totems, ancestors, and the like. You may receive information, clarity, and guidance that proves to be astonishingly accurate.

Facing Your Demons

As psychedelics soften psychological defenses and cut through denial, you may unearth scary "demons" from traumatic childhood memories that expose the truth about your family, your childhood, and yourself.

During your session, your guide will encourage you to focus beyond your thoughts, into your breath and body. Parts of your body may vibrate, feel tingly, electric, warm, and alive. Other parts may feel painful, tense, heavy, numb, or jittery. You may become cold, nauseous, dizzy, feverish, or drowsy. Your breathing and heartbeat may quicken, you may shiver, your teeth may chatter, you might have the urge to urinate, defecate, vomit, or flee. If this happens, you know you are right on the edge of accessing buried trauma that is ready to be felt and released. If scary, painful feelings or traumatic memories surface, your guide will help you safely through them.

As your breathing softens muscular armor, your body may involuntarily tremble, spasm, or thrash about. You might belch, wretch, or vomit. Your legs might kick or run in place. Your hands may clench into fists that pound or punch. Your arms may make pushing-away movements or protective gestures. These are thwarted fight or flight impulses that were frozen with the trauma. These spontaneous, instinctual actions allow the body to discharge trauma.

During your session, the full impact of old emotional wounds may be felt and released in cathartic explosions of grief, rage, or terror. You may regress to an earlier age, engulfed in vivid, sensory experiences of repressed traumatic events. You may experience the intense emotional pain of feeling unloved by caretakers. You might feel the physical pain of rape, injuries, abuse, surgery, etc. as if it were happening now. As the pain, fear, and anger are felt and released, old wounds heal. The supportive, therapeutic setting allows you to safely feel emotions you've run from for many years.

Mourning

As you come out of the shock of trauma, you may need to grieve the absence of the protection, love, and caring you needed as a child. You'll need time to nurture and comfort your wounded self. While you are in an open, altered state, and still somewhat regressed, you may receive from your caring sitter some of the love and comfort you didn't get from your family. If you are in a receptive mood, this can have the effect of reprogramming unmet childhood needs for attention, acceptance, respect, understanding, and tender touch.

When the trauma has been fully felt, discharged, and grieved, the protective walls you built around your heart will melt. You will now be able to love and let love in deeply. You will feel lighter, calmer, and happier. Addictions, depression, neuroses, psychosomatic medical issues, and self-defeating patterns of behavior will fall away. You will be drawn into relationships that are deeply loving and without painful drama. You will now be able to love and care for yourself enough to create a life where the deepest needs of your heart and soul are met.

The Hero's Journey

The healing process is much like a mythological Hero's Journey. Shaken from complacency by a crisis or intolerable suffering, you begin the quest for a cure. You meet a guide, swallow an elixir, close your eyes, and plunge down the rabbit hole into a mysterious inner world. You face fears, discover enchanted realms, enlist allies, and conquer demons.

There is no single Yellow Brick Road to follow. Once begun, your healing journey unfolds with its own unique, organic intelligence. Your first steps may be full of beauty and wonder as you discover ethereal realms of consciousness beyond the ordinary. Visiting these realms gives you glimpses of vast, unexplored, inner landscapes.

On your quest for healing, you will eventually encounter domains of darkness whose gates are guarded by the fierce demons of your fears. When you are strong and ready for the task, you walk through your fears and begin the descent into hidden pain and trauma at the core of your being.

Each psychedelic session may reveal a new layer of previously repressed trauma which must be acknowledged, felt and integrated. You may find many layers of fear, anger, and sadness arising from various periods of your life. The more intense and prolonged your trauma, and the earlier in childhood your wounding occurred, the longer your trek through darkness may be.

For some, a few sessions can be life changing; for others the healing journey may be a long and winding road. If you surrender to the process, taking time to rest and recharge after each encounter, you will come through into the light. The pain and trauma that was stored in your body and psyche is finite. Once felt and discharged, you are forever free of it.

As old wounds are peeled away, you uncover a radiant Self that has been healed and transformed by the Hero's Journey. You emerge from the adventure happier, stronger, and wiser.

4. PRIMARY TOOLS

There are many useful therapeutic tools in the psychedelic pharmacopeia. This section discusses four basic substances: MDMA (ecstasy), LSD, psilocybin (magic mushrooms), and marijuana. Each has unique benefits and unique limitations. They can be calibrated by dosage, they can be enhanced, and they can be combined, depending on the journeyer's needs at the time of the session. With patience and skilled, intelligent use, these four materials can facilitate the healing of most psychological wounds.

Psychedelics by themselves have no intrinsic, magical healing properties. The therapeutic effectiveness of these drugs depends on the intention, emotional state, mental health, personal history, and level of awareness of the user. The effectiveness of these drugs is also enhanced by the safety, privacy, and aesthetics of the setting, and the caliber of the sitter/therapist.

The efficacy of each drug in an individual's healing process may vary. What works well in one person's therapy may not work the same way for someone else. Extremely wounded people with thick walls of defenses may initially have disappointingly limited experiences.

Dosages generally need to be adjusted to fit the body weight and gender of the journeyer. Men often need higher doses than women.

Less guarded individuals with sensitive constitutions may need lower doses.

Moderate doses are safest and generally most suitable for psychedelic-assisted psychotherapy. The term "psycholytic therapy" has been used to describe this conservative dose protocol. High dose work will not be covered in this guide.

MDMA (Ecstasy)

MDMA is a relatively mild, highly controllable feeling enhancer. It's ideal for working with emotional issues and trauma. It softens feelings of fear and shame, allowing journeyers to speak honestly and openly about painful or embarrassing issues they may never have felt safe to disclose before--even to themselves.

MDMA relaxes chronic psychological defenses. It engulfs the subject in warm feelings that promote trust and open communication. It speeds the development of a healing, therapeutic bond between the journeyer and the sitter or therapist. This effect of MDMA also makes it ideal for couples counseling.

MDMA's famous "ecstatic" experience of feeling good, relaxed, open, peaceful, and present in one's body can be revelatory for very wounded people who cannot remember ever having known such a pleasant state. Psychologically healthy human beings often feel relaxed, open, and peaceful just naturally. MDMA gives the journeyer a glimpse of this end goal of therapeutic work. Neurotic and psychosomatic symptoms are often temporarily suspended during the journey. Inhibitions and self-conscious behaviors fall away. Defensive body armor, constrictions, and chronically tight muscles soften.

The chatter of the analytical mind quiets and allows the rich, satisfying experience of being fully present in the moment. Journeyers can experience a taste of the way life feels when their trauma has been released and their human potential is no longer blocked. They can find themselves in a profound serenity that resembles the state of samadhi, a mental and emotional condition that disciplined meditators practice years to achieve. As this state becomes imprinted and integrated into consciousness, it can become familiar and more accessible using non-drug relaxation methods.

MDMA promotes uninhibited, honest communication. It allows journeyers to relax into a positive experience of genuine intimacy that can be learned and incorporated into daily life. For those who have been isolated inside their own emotional walls, this oceanic experience of love and openness offers an opportunity to feel the pleasure of being connected to others. It may motivate them to begin healing important relationships and fashioning permanent doors in their emotional walls.

MDMA magnifies awareness of body sensations, thoughts, emotions, and intuitive perceptions that are normally repressed, unconscious, or ignored. From this expanded perspective, fresh insights into deep-rooted issues may emerge.

Therapeutically used, MDMA is a powerful tool that can melt psychological defenses and break the spell of denial and amnesia that keeps people in the dark about the existence, source, or intensity of prior trauma. Engulfed in a state of well-being, freed of fear and shame, the journeyer is able, without being overwhelmed, to vividly recall, feel, and release the primal terror, pain, and rage of forgotten trauma.

MDMA does not pierce as deeply through some of the veils of denial as other psychedelics. Sometimes it will be too euphoric and shield the journeyer from deeper layers of trauma. At that point, continuing to work with MDMA, alone or mixed with other psychedelics, may abort deeper healing. It may sugar-coat shadow material that needs to be experienced raw in order to fully heal. If a journeyer is given more MDMA later in a session when they are getting close to significant trauma, the healing process may be derailed. MDMA is an amazing tool for lowering defenses and fear levels when needed, but it can sometimes mask old pain, anger, and fear that needs to be felt and discharged.

Other times, MDMA may not soften the psychedelic therapy experience. Those who are sitting on trauma that is ready to surface may not experience the pleasurable, soothing qualities for which MDMA is famous.

For most people, an effective dose is around 100 milligrams. A single dose will provide a working period of about four hours. Augmenting the initial dose with an additional dose of 50 to 100 mg about an hour later will insure an optimal, effective working period of five to six hours. The strength of the booster dose should be determined by how responsive the journeyer is to the original dose.

Tolerance can be a significant problem with MDMA. Unlike LSD and psilocybin, MDMA will lose effectiveness if used too often or too long. To extend its useful therapeutic lifespan with a given journeyer, no more than 200 mg should be administered in a single session, and at least two weeks should elapse between MDMA sessions.

One must exercise discipline to get the most out of MDMA. Exceeding the maximum recommended dosage of 200 milligrams is likely to create unpleasant side effects that overwhelm any good that might have been achieved in the session. Also, using MDMA more than once every two weeks will quickly lead to the development of tolerance, after which the benefits decline and die out.

Common side effects of MDMA use are appetite loss, jaw clenching, and nystagmus (lateral eye wiggle). The use of calcium-magnesium supplements the day before and leading up to the use of MDMA helps decrease jaw tension. This can prevent days of soreness for individuals who chronically hold tension in their jaws.

A journeyer may feel substantially depleted for one or more days after an MDMA session. It may be difficult to sleep. Their jaws may be tight or painful, or they could feel tired or depressed. Therefore, to the extent possible, journeyers should clear their schedule of demanding work and difficult personal encounters for up to three days after the session.

Some people claim that taking 100 mg of 5-HTP (available in health food stores) each day for three days before a session and for four to six days afterward helps avoid the serotonin dip that causes the MDMA hangover. Do not take 5-HTP less than six hours before a journey.

Contraction often follows the emotional and sensory expansion provided by MDMA. Returning to something like their previously contracted state can be discouraging for journeyers, who may think no progress has been made. The body's contraction after a huge expansion is normal and healthy. It's a return to the boundaries that help a person navigate a complex social and economic world. But it can feel overwhelmingly sad and depressing when contrasted with memories of the expanded MDMA experience. Journeyers should be advised beforehand that they may feel down and depressed for a couple of days after the MDMA experience, and that it may take a few days to notice ways they have become more open and functional as a result of their session.

Persons with the following conditions should avoid taking MDMA or use only a very small dose: heart conditions, high blood pressure, diabetes, and bipolar disorder.

Persons taking certain medications should avoid concurrent use of MDMA. MDMA should not be used by anyone taking an MAO inhibitor, fluvoxamine (sold as Fevarin, etc.), or ritonavir (aka Norvir).

SSRI antidepressants must be discontinued gradually starting at least six weeks prior to an MDMA session. (It's extremely dangerous to stop taking an SSRI abruptly.) A person must be completely off SSRIs for at least two weeks before an MDMA session.

Some over-the-counter cough, cold, and asthma medicines may present problems with MDMA use, such as pseudoephedrine (Sudafed), and dextromethorphan (or DXM, in Robitussin, NyQuil and others). As a precaution, intake of these medications should be stopped or strictly limited prior to MDMA usage. More information is available at https://dancesafe.org/drug-information/mdma-contraindications/.

LSD

In psychotherapy, LSD's most salient quality is to greatly amplify whatever is hidden in one's unconscious. It cuts right through trance and denial. LSD allows vivid access to buried memories like being in mother's womb, birth trauma, infantile trauma, and early childhood physical and sexual abuse memories that are difficult or impossible to retrieve through other means.

LSD allows access to previously blocked aspects of the inner worlds of body, psyche, and spirit. With eyes closed, one can experience a whole universe of sensations inside the body. Focusing on problem areas in the body can reveal psychosomatic roots of pain, malfunction, and disease.

LSD promotes clarity. It's a powerful, versatile tool that lets journeyers focus directly into the heart of their issues. It encourages creative, innovative thinking and out-of-the-box problem solving.

Like a truth serum, LSD has the capacity to awaken one from lifelong trance states that were induced by early trauma or harmful familial and cultural beliefs. New concepts and profound realizations can be accepted and absorbed, replacing erroneous core beliefs about the self, others, the world, reality, life, and death.

At higher doses, LSD opens doors to transcendent dimensions of reality, transgenerational memories, and unresolved trauma from previous lifetimes.

LSD is not usually the best therapeutic choice for intellectuals and other head-trippers. It may create the illusion that thinking can solve everything.

Overdosing with LSD can be overwhelming, dangerous, and retraumatizing. The higher the dose, the more likely both sitter and journeyer will get into scary, hard-to-manage territory. The potential for inadvertently causing psychological harm at higher doses requires that the sitter be experienced and extremely knowledgeable.

Unlike MDMA, LSD has no inherent feel-good properties. Those who have significant childhood trauma may find LSD to be stark and brutal in higher doses. High doses may sometimes plummet these journeyers into abstract, paranoid mind spaces where everything seems fake and godless.

The higher the dose of LSD, the more it may amplify negative transference. Hatred or fear originally felt toward some perpetrator, parent, etc., may be transferred onto the therapist/sitter. In the journeyer's mind, the sitter becomes the feared or hated person from the past, and all safety vanishes from the setting. Having a second or backup sitter, preferably of a different gender, can save the day.

Getting lost in trippy visuals or music may be a defense against deeper exploration. Breathing deeply and continuously help a journeyer keep from getting caught in the shallows. Higher doses of LSD may last eight or nine hours. A session this long will exhaust even the most intrepid sitter.

Even small amounts of LSD have powerful effects. Most beginners should start with a 100 mcg dose. Starting with a low dose, the journeyer can cautiously work up to higher doses in future journeys, if needed. When used by itself, or as the primary tool for a session, the dosage will likely range from 50 to 300 mcg. A moderate dose will provide an effective working period of six to eight hours. Higher doses generally last longer. Some prescription medications are contraindicated when taking LSD. Check with erowid.org or another reliable source for information.

For many, the after-effects of LSD can be jarring or jagged. Sleep may be difficult the first night without some form of assisted relaxation, such as melatonin or valerian.

Psilocybin (Magic Mushrooms)

Magic mushrooms are all-purpose, shamanic medicine teachers that seem to have their own organic intelligence. They are catalysts that promote accelerated personal healing, awareness, and spiritual growth in ways that are uniquely relevant to each sincere seeker. The intelligence of the mushrooms appears to interface with one's own deepest wisdom, bringing forth whatever experience is most beneficial for healing and awakening at the time of the journey.

Psilocybin powerfully and relentlessly unlocks the doors to an individual's deeper truth. Anything that is blocked, constricted, unconscious, or out of integrity will be brought to conscious awareness. This may not be a pleasant experience, but it results in profound, liberating change.

For some, memories and reenactments of hidden trauma surface as if they are happening for the first time in that moment. The expansive nature of psilocybin promotes physical and emotional release of trauma. As the nervous system releases suppressed fight and flight impulses, the body may involuntarily thrash about, shake, spasm, kick, hit, twist, etc. There may be deep emotional catharsis like sobbing or screaming. Some journeyers sob for hours, feeling previously unexpressed grief for their own pain and the pain of all beings who suffer.

Certain transpersonal experiences, which may also occur with LSD, are more common with psilocybin. Some people experience a state of pure, peaceful being, and deep wisdom without thought or identification with their ego self. Some feel their interconnection with all beings and a sense of oneness with nature. Some receive guidance from a source beyond their rational mind. In higher doses, psilocybin can open up realms beyond the ego mind, beyond space and time, beyond the personal unconscious into the collective unconscious realms of numinous archetypes and spirit. Some people report accessing cellular memory of being earlier evolutionary life forms, being a sperm or an egg, reliving intrauterine or past life experiences, or experiencing unhealed trauma from their parents and ancestors.

Like LSD, psilocybin can awaken one from personal and cultural trance. Liberation from limiting beliefs can inspire expansion into one's full potential, and free one to explore creative, fulfilling lifestyles beyond society's straitjacket of conventions.

Sometimes journeys are sprinkled with childlike giggling and laughter. One may be able to appreciate the Cosmic Joke--seeing the humor in our lives, our culture, and the human condition. Laughter can be a joyous, cathartic release, and a doorway to the happy inner child.

Psilocybin seems to have its own organic, healing intelligence. While this trait is magical, it makes psilocybin an unwieldy medicine that can seldom be focused onto a particular issue. It's not amenable to much direction by the journeyer's will or by the therapist/ sitter. Once it's ingested, personal control and psychotherapeutic paradigms are best abandoned. Psilocybin may not give the experience most desired, but it will generally give the experience most needed. The best way to approach a mushroom journey is to imagine laying on an operating room table, surrendering to the wisdom of the Great Surgeon.

Psilocybin can promote dissociation at higher doses. Moderate doses are needed when the intention is to stay embodied and focused on trauma releasing.

Most beginners should start with a 3-gram dose of dried mushrooms. This dose can be gradually increased to 6-9 grams in future journeys, if needed. The lowest dose that can be felt is between 1 and 2 grams. A single dose provides an effective working period of three to six hours.

An accurate scale is essential to measure fractions of a gram. The difference between one gram and two of mushrooms cannot be distinguished by sight, but will be felt clearly once ingested. The potency may vary from batch to batch.

Mushrooms can be eaten but many people dislike the taste. They are somewhat more palatable ground to a powder in a coffee grinder and mixed in a blender with juice. Pineapple-grapefruit juice works well. They can also be brewed into a tea.

Here is one recipe: Chop mushrooms up into 1/4 inch chunks. Soak chunks for 15 minutes in just enough lemon juice to cover. Drain juice and save. Add boiling water, and steep mushrooms for 20 minutes.

Discard mushrooms. Mix the tea with the lemon juice and add a little maple syrup or other sweetener.

Psilocybin may promote nausea. Slight nausea is common, especially at the beginning of a journey. More intense nausea usually indicates that scary, upsetting feelings or unconscious material is coming up to be healed. After psilocybin has been digested and absorbed--about an hour or so--vomiting should be allowed. Throwing up is one way the body releases trauma. The journeyer usually feels much better afterwards. This sort of purging can promote lasting, positive life changes.

Higher doses (five to ten grams) may cause temporary loss of touch with reality, highly amplified transference, and delusional thinking, usually during the peak hour of the journey. This may manifest as bizarre, unsafe behavior like wanting to fly off a balcony or believing the sitter is Hitler.

The higher the dose, the less likely one may remember what happened during the journey. This does not affect results. Higher doses may also trigger an "ego death" phenomenon in which subjects seriously believe they are dying or going permanently crazy. Navigating through such an experience in a safe, supportive setting can be transformational. For more information, read the "Beyond Ego" section in this guide.

The higher the dose, the more likely both sitter and subject can get into scary, unwieldy territory. The risk of inadvertently causing psychological harm requires that the sitter be experienced and extremely knowledgeable when high doses of psilocybin are being used.

Marijuana

In a therapeutic setting, where the intention of emotional healing is clear and strong, smoking marijuana is a shorter-acting, milder option that can work in ways similar to psychedelics. This is an especially effective option for journeyers who have not established a pattern of using marijuana recreationally or to self-medicate. Once psychedelics have opened the doors to a person's unconscious, judicious use of marijuana away from the psychedelic session can continue the healing process. For some people, pot helps access feelings, insights, and buried trauma.

Smoking pot during a psychedelic therapy session is seldom a good idea. It tends to promote dissociation, fuzziness, and loss of focus. However, at the end of a journey, when the journeyer needs to let go and rest, marijuana may help bring on a much-needed period of relaxation and pleasure.

Edible Marijuana

Indica strains of cannabis greatly amplify awareness of bodily sensations. This medicine allows those who habitually live in their heads to feel their bodies. Whereas it's common for psychedelics to bring up trauma, this is less likely to happen with marijuana.

Marijuana cooked into butter, candy, cookies, brownies and other food items is particularly helpful for this. Take care not to overdose on edibles! Excessive doses can induce harrowing experiences. Potency of edibles varies greatly, and it may be hours before it's evident how any given amount will affect a journeyer.

Start experimenting with lower doses. If more is needed, it's possible to gradually work up to edibles containing four to eight grams of pot. Even if eaten on an empty stomach, it may be an hour and a half before their effects are felt, if at all. After that, effects will strengthen, then continue for five or six hours.

Mixing Medicines

In a session in which LSD is to be the principal tool, an initial dose of 70-100 mg of MDMA, taken about an hour before the LSD, creates a softer entry for new users into the world of the stronger medicine. Similarly, when psilocybin is to be the principal tool, one may lead with a single dose of MDMA a half-hour to an hour before the psilocybin. For journeyers who already have a good relationship with MDMA, this is an ideal way to gently introduce new and unfamiliar substances.

If a journeyer using LSD or psilocybin alone starts having difficulty letting go of their defenses and relaxing into the experience, administering MDMA may allow them to proceed fearlessly into deeper territory. Or if they get stuck in a dark place, and are unable to process through it, administering MDMA at that point may facilitate a gentle finish that will not leave them in a negative psychological state. For those who are emotionally shut down, adding MDMA to the other psychedelic may promote a more heart-opening experience. Finally, putting MDMA in the mix with LSD or psilocybin can help a chronically anxious and internally constricted journeyer relax and open up.

When using LSD and MDMA together, adding LSD amps up the intensity of an MDMA session. It introduces more clarity, and it promotes breaking through denial and amnesia to an extent that MDMA alone might not achieve.

Combining psilocybin with LSD is a particularly effective protocol for accessing and releasing trauma. Taking LSD about an hour before ingesting psilocybin breaks through denial and brings up buried traumatic memories. Adding the softening, healing properties of psilocybin induces the release of the trauma from the body. This powerful combination is not for beginners in psychedelic therapy.

LSD and Edible Marijuana is useful for people who have been dissociated from their bodies all their life, either through constant thinking or through spacing out. Relatively low doses of LSD (generally not more than 150 mcg) combined with Indica-strain edible cannabis is an excellent tool for helping them explore and get grounded into their bodies.

Introducing New Medicines Gradually

MDMA is an ideal, safe medicine for first journeys. Its gentle nature allows inexperienced beginners to become comfortable exploring non-ordinary states of consciousness. If you are an experienced recreational user of MDMA and other psychedelic meds, using psychedelics to explore deep-seated psychological issues in a therapeutic setting may be surprisingly uncomfortable and challenging. Don't assume, just because psychedelics were always pleasant when you used them recreationally, that using them for therapy will be a walk in the park. Start with MDMA.

Depending on your own unique circumstances and issues, MDMA journeys may allow you to resolve all the issues for which you came to therapy. If it's working, there's no need to change it. If, however, you have not been able to reach your therapeutic goals with MDMA, and you and your sitter feel that you're ready to go deeper, you can gradually introduce small amounts of mushrooms and/or LSD into your journeys. At first you might begin these deeper sessions with 100 mg or less of MDMA to soften defenses and anxiety about the unfamiliar meds. This will help you relax and let go into the new experience. Alternatively, you may want to try a low dose of each new medicine by itself, so you can gain familiarity with its unique properties and capabilities.

It's important to go slowly. Introduce stronger medicines gradually. While it might take a few journeys to work up to the dose that will be most effective for you, being gentle and cautious will prevent the re-traumatization that results if you push too far, too fast. One consequence of going too fast is that you may be afraid to return to journeywork again. There is often a vast difference between what your mind thinks you can handle and what your psyche can actually handle. Fools rush in where wise ones fear to tread. If you've had a harrowing LSD or psilocybin journey that felt like you bit off more than you could chew, lower the dose and reintroduce MDMA into your next journey to softly navigate through the trauma of the previous, overwhelming journey.

If you are successfully working through trauma or accessing buried pain, it's not helpful to add more medicines late in the journey to extend the session. The psyche seems able to handle only one chunk of difficult material at a time.

5. USING A SITTER

If you are contemplating doing this therapy, you will want to work with a skilled practitioner experienced in the field of psychedelic healing.

Therapeutic journeywork will and should be very different from recreational trips you may have experienced. Any thought that you are experienced enough to embark on this kind of journey without assistance is naive. The fact that you are contemplating journeywork for healing is a strong indicator that there are hidden, unexplored places in your psyche, filled with things you've been avoiding because you couldn't handle seeing them. It's foolish to imagine you'll know what to do when you face your own unconscious and long-hidden material for the first time in journeyspace. If disturbing feelings and memories surface, an experienced sitter will help you move safely through them.

A competent sitter can reassure journeyers and support them as they process through emerging sensations, feelings, visions, and behaviors that may be bizarre, incomprehensible, or scary. A wise practitioner can help you make sense of your sometimes wild and crazy experience. Your mind craves and needs such clarity for it to be an ally in your healing process.

Your eyes are part of your face, so you can't see your face without a mirror. Similarly, you'll need a sitter to direct your awareness and attention to patterns, symptoms, and blind spots that you can't see yourself.

Your psychological defenses will be challenged during journeywork. Defenses block you from getting to difficult, core material that needs healing. A sitter sees what's happening and helps you navigate through your defenses in a way that you, in journeyspace, would be unable to do.

It's easy to get lost in journeyspace. A sitter can help you keep track. An idea, a thought, a discussion that you want to follow, may just slip from your mind. "What was I saying?" comes up more often that you might think.

Journeywork may bring up repressed emotional pain and trauma from events long ago that no one ever talked about or perhaps even knew about. Having an empathic witness to see, hear, and validate your experience is itself part of the healing.

It's comforting to let go and rely on someone else to take care of you. While in an altered state, you may need help getting water, getting to the bathroom, getting an extra blanket, and other tactical maneuvers. Your sitter will assist you when needed. A sitter will also handle any unexpected emergencies and glitches like audio equipment malfunctions, power outages, a clogged toilet, etc.

A sitter can run interference for you, shielding you from unwanted, unexpected guests that might show up in the middle of a journey. Besides totally derailing whatever was going on in your journey, these interruptions can be scary and debilitating. A trustworthy sitter will handle any unforeseen danger or distraction so that you can relax and let your full attention be absorbed in your inner experience.

Meet with your sitter for at least an hour or two on a day prior to your journey. Make sure your sitter knows as much as possible about you, your issues, and your history. The sitter must agree to keep confidential your information and everything that happens during the journey. Take this time to share your fears about doing journeywork and any concerns about working with your sitter, regardless of how silly or insignificant they seem.

Sharing journeyspace with a sitter provides an opportunity to connect with and practice being open, vulnerable, and totally honest with an attentive, caring, non-judgmental human being. The relationship with the sitter becomes a safe space in which your interpersonal issues can emerge and heal.

In a hundred ways, a skilled, experienced practitioner can help you step around the many potholes and dangerous road conditions that come up in journeys. Sitters will have knowledge, tools, and techniques that enable them to make precise interventions and comments to help you in your healing. Effective guides will have done extensive work on healing their own trauma and will be both knowledgeable and experienced in psychotherapeutic and altered state shadow work. Having a competent guide will substantially reduce the chance of your becoming retraumatized, which could leave you with the kind of damage that causes some people to turn their backs on this powerful mode of therapy.

The use of the substances described in these pages is presently illegal in the USA and in many other countries. You will therefore find little in the way of advertising by practitioners in the field. Word of mouth is the most effective way to find a good sitter. Alternative healing practitioners are more likely than most to have encountered someone who does this kind of work.

6. GUIDELINES FOR THE SITTER

You, as sitter, are performing an essential service. The journeyer is depending on you in deep and critical ways. If you are careless, inexperienced, or uninformed, you can cause serious psychological damage. What you do and say can have a profound effect on the outcome of the journey. Therefore, it is important that you review and fully understand these guidelines.

Most of the healing that takes place will come from within the journeyer. A vast reservoir of healing intelligence resides within each person. Psychedelics allow that reservoir to open. Sitters must step back and allow journeyers to discover and follow their own inner wisdom and guidance.

Every journey path is unique. If you have done journeywork yourself but have never been a sitter for others, you may expect and coax others to have experiences like yours. That would be a mistake. It's essential that you, as sitter, completely let go of personal agendas and rigid therapeutic formulas in order to support each journeyer's individual process. You must fearlessly accommodate new situations that may not fit any conventional theoretical framework.

You must rigorously monitor any personal ego desires to be

validated as a clever, knowledgeable guide. Avoid any temptation to play guru or brilliant therapist. Let the healing process unfold out of the journeyer's own inner direction and authority.

Being a sitter is more of an art form than a science. While knowledge and experience are crucial, an ideal sitter needs to be sensitive, caring, and intuitive. A sitter's job is mostly passive. However, sometimes judicious intervention or involvement is necessary.

This section assumes that the intended sitter has little or no experience in sitting for another's journey. However, many of the guidelines and suggestions will also be useful to the more experienced sitter.

Keeping It Safe

First and foremost, the sitter is present to insure that the journeyer does not get hurt or damage the journey setting. A journeyer who is releasing trauma may thrash about wildly or need to discharge anger by hitting something. The sitter should provide a punching bag or pillows to accommodate anger release, and make sure nothing in the room gets damaged.

Suicidal or self-destructive impulses may occasionally arise during the journey of one who has been deeply traumatized. They may feel driven to hit or claw themselves, pull their hair, hit their head against a wall, etc. If the conduct could produce real injury, you should express concern and stop the self-harming impulses from being acted out. You might communicate, in a compassionate way, something like: "You've been hurt enough already. Please don't hurt yourself."

The desire to die or feel physical pain is normally a defense against a frighteningly painful emotion or memory that is trying to come up. The fact that this underlying material is surfacing in the journey is good, because that means it's ready to be released. But the journeyer must be guided past self-destructive thoughts and be reassured that they are now an adult who is strong enough to face whatever comes up. A period of slow, regular breathing can help journeyers move past fear-based, self-destructive impulses and open them to the feeling or memory that's trying to come through.

Sexual Boundaries

NEVER ALLOW ANYTHING SEXUAL TO HAPPEN BETWEEN THE JOURNEYER AND THE SITTER.

There's a very high statistical likelihood that a journeyer's psychological problems may be traced back to some form of sexual abuse or other sexual boundary violation in their past. This may be true even when journeyers have no memory of abuse or reason to suspect that any sexual trauma has ever happened to them. Because they have been abused, or because they are in an altered state, journeyers may have no sense of appropriate sexual boundaries. It's up to you to make sure those boundaries are never crossed for any reason.

As sitter, you are in the position of a protective, caring parent to the journeyer. Even if he or she becomes seductive, asks you to participate in sexual healing, says they want or need this and know what they are doing, do NOT cross the sexual boundary. The reality is, this journeyer may be acting out past sexual trauma. Letting that happen in journeyspace would cause re-traumatization and would permanently, irrevocably disrupt the relationship of trust and safety between sitter and journeyer. If a journeyer is being seductive, remind them in a kind way that there is a rule against any kind of sexual contact between you.

For some people who have been deeply damaged, sexual engagement feels like the only way they can connect to others or to their own worth. They think their only value lies in their sexual desirability. To validate this destructive belief would do great harm. Explain that you understand the journeyer may believe they have to be desired to be valued, but that's not really true. Name the journeyer's best traits, such as intelligence, sensitivity, talent, or courage, and say something like, "I admire these traits in you and hope you will come to see how valuable you are because of them."

Appropriate hugging, holding, and non-sexual touching can be hugely healing in journeyspace. As sitter, you must always ask the journeyer's permission before initiating any sort of physical contact. There should be an agreement that if the journeyer starts to feel uncomfortable, contact from the sitter will stop or change as requested.

You must be rigorously vigilant to be sure that your physical contact with the journeyer does not come from your own needs or desires.

There is a line that you, as sitter, should never cross. If you don't know where that line is, or if you feel you could be tempted to cross that line, decline right up front to sit for the journeyer. If you are journeying with a significant other with whom you have an established, trusting sexual relationship, the line will be different than with a casual acquaintance or friend. The ability of psychedelics to bypass shame, suppress inhibitions, soften body armor, amplify sensual stimuli, and rewire neural pleasure pathways in the brain can make them highly effective in sexual healing work. Until you've had experience doing journeywork together without sexual touch, however, you might not recognize the risks you are taking.

The journey setting needs to be a safe, confidential, non-shaming space where natural eroticism is celebrated and journeyers feel free to talk openly about sex. They need to be able to discuss fantasies, desires, inhibitions, and to confess shameful or deviant sexual attractions or behaviors. They may need to feel their own genitals or get naked. As sitter, you must never impose your own sexual morals, sex-negative beliefs, judgments, or hang-ups on the journeyer.

On rare occasions, a journeyer may feel a genuine need to explore their own genitals or masturbate in order to heal early sexual shaming or to consciously inhabit their genitals. Be sure the journeyer is using masturbation to heal, and not to escape disturbing feelings or memories that are coming up in the work. If the person is a sex addict, they may habitually masturbate to avoid facing their feelings. Don't let that happen in journeyspace; focus them back on the experience they were having when the desire to masturbate came up. If the journeyer is not acting out sexual addiction or using the sitter as an object of desire, this impulse should be allowed within mutually comfortable boundaries. For example, you can drape a sheet over the journeyer, you may turn your back, or you may temporarily leave the room.

Presence

Journeyers whose feelings and thoughts were not seen, heard, or taken seriously when they were children, will need your complete attention and emotional attunement. This makes journeyspace a deeply corrective experience in which the journeyer feels supported by a completely available, patient, interested, accepting, surrogate parent. This helps them develop a sense of self-worth, and it opens up their ability to receive from others.

In journeyspace, those who feel self-conscious and anxious relating to others can learn to relax and feel confident in the presence of an amicable sitter. The sitter must be authentic and sincere. In an altered state, journeyers can easily detect false comments and demeanor.

Your presence as sitter is important for the journey as a whole, but there may be times when the journeyer will want privacy. Honoring that is part of being a good surrogate parent. If it seems safe to do so, you may agree to leave the room for a while. The journeyer can call you back in when ready, or there can be an agreement for you to check back in after a period of time.

Focusing Coach

One of the sitter's jobs is to keep the journeyer from intellectualizing, spacing out, or avoiding uncomfortable issues and feelings. Sometimes, journeyers will ask the sitter to help them focus; more often, the sitter will have to sense when there's a need for it and take the initiative.

Beginning journeyers often believe they must cognitively monitor and understand what's going on during the session in order to heal. They may need frequent coaching to suspend their mind's need to know, and to trust the inner intelligence of their body and psyche. The time to analyze and think about the experience is after the journey is over.

Many journeyers process feelings and memories by talking about them as they come up. This can go on for hours, and it's fine. But constant talking that reflects thinking or figuring things out intellectually can be an avoidance tactic rather than a method of processing. If it looks like that's what's going on, try focusing the journeyer's attention on their breath and into their body. You can also remind them that thinking gets in the way of feeling, and feeling is the true guide on a journey.

Journeyers who have caretaker or co-dependent tendencies may need reminding to stay focused on themselves, rather than get distracted about fixing other people.

Journeyers could have a hard time surrendering into an altered state. Or they may become stuck in a fearful place during the journey and not be able to move forward. At these times, you may need to offer frequent reassurance, saying, "It's okay; you're safe. I'm here holding your hand." You may also remind them they can trust the wisdom of the medicine, their body, and their Higher Self.

During difficult parts of the journey, you will likely need to coach the journeyer to breathe fully. Deep, deliberate, steady breathing carries the journeyer past fear and thinking, deep into the truth and the healing spaces of the unconscious. Coach the journeyer with gentle, verbal reminders to breathe or remind them to breathe by breathing out loud yourself.

When journeyers suddenly get nauseous, or drift off into thinking or daydreaming, it generally means they're close to traumatic memories they are afraid to explore. Motivate journeyers to persevere by informing them that they are approaching a valuable healing opportunity. Get them back on course by urging them to breathe. Let them know they are strong enough now to handle whatever comes up.

Right in the middle of recovering a traumatic memory, a journeyer may space out and forget what just happened or where they are in the unfolding memory. They may need reminders and coaching to focus them back into the experience. You can ask questions like, "What happens next?" "Who is in the room with you?" "How old do you feel?" "Is it daytime or nighttime?" and so on.

People who were physically, sexually or verbally abused as children often learned to dissociate or "space out" to escape the pain of their experience. When that pain starts to be remembered or felt in journeyspace, it's essential that they stay present in their body to feel, process and release it, as opposed to denying or escaping it. Some sort of physical contact, massage, or bodywork may help them stay grounded, but be sure you ask first if it's okay to touch them. If touching would interfere, you can coach journeyers to rub their arms or legs, or stretch, or bicycle their legs in the air, whatever keeps them feeling that they are in a body.

A person's body will often signal where trauma is stored by creating physical pain in that place. So if someone shows up for a journey talking about how stiff their hip is or how tight they feel around their heart, take note. Take note also if they become suddenly aware of a physical pain during the journey. In either case, help the journeyer focus attention into the painful place. With sustained attention, the sensation of pain can become a guide into a trauma that has been buried in the body for many years. Coach the journeyer to stay focused and breathe into the pain. A sitter might say something like, " The pain is a part of you that's like a hurt little child. It needs your love and attention in order to feel better. Imagine that with each inhale you are sending fresh oxygen and healing into the pain." If the journeyer finds it hard to maintain focus, you might ask about the size and intensity of the pain or if it has a color, an emotion, a message, or any visual image or words coming from it.

Coaching is best communicated as reminders and suggestions, not commands. A sitter might say something like, "You might try experimenting with focusing your attention into the painful place and explore what you find there." To avoid performance anxiety in journeyers who are new to this type of work, the sitter can suggest that they may or may not find something to experience by focusing into the painful place.

If it becomes clear that the journeyer is not yet ready to focus, the sitter should respect the person's natural pace and let it go for a while. After having some time to digress, talk, joke, or follow their own inner guidance, journeyers may be more ready to tackle the defended, scary places.

If a person is having a difficult journey, they might be feeling more terror, anguish, and emotional pain than they've ever felt in their life. Their body may involuntarily spasm, shake, or thrash about. This is a healing process, but it won't feel that way to them! They'll need the sitter's calming reassurance that this is a cathartic release of stuff they've been holding in their bodies. Let journeyers know that if they allow themselves to really feel it, they are moving through it, processing it, and letting it go forever. The more trauma they allow themselves to feel now, the lighter and happier they'll be for the rest of their life.

It may be helpful for the sitter to explain that being willing to surrender to these hellish feelings is like moving through a long, dark tunnel. Let them know that if they stay with the feelings, they will eventually come out into the light on the other side. After many hours of an arduous, turbulent shadow journey, there will usually be a positive shift into a rewarding, peaceful experience. Often this happens toward the end of a journey; other times it may show up in the next few days.

When journeyers are experiencing trauma, your job as sitter is first and foremost to stay calm. Anything you see is OK. Don't try to stop or fix the experience. Let it play out. Inspire the journeyer to keep going. You may need to offer reassurance, soothing touch, and a sense of safety during challenging moments. You can support them through difficult episodes with phrases such as these:

"You are safe, now. It's safe to feel these feelings."

"These are old feelings. You're not in danger here and now."

"Keep breathing and feeling. You're doing great work."

"You're being really brave to feel these feelings. You're getting through a lot."

"Stay with it, keep going."

"You will get through this; you are stronger than you think."

If it's clear the journeyer is becoming overwhelmed, you might say something like, "You have control over these feelings. You can take a break, if you really need to."

A journeyer may sometimes become very still and quiet for long periods of time. They're not falling asleep, but are seemingly engrossed in some inner world. A lot of good work may be going on inside, and it's best not to interrupt that. Generally people move out of it on their own. But the stillness may also suggest a dissociated (spaced-out) state, in which no healing work is being done. If you're not sure if the journeyer is spacing out or deeply engaged in a productive experience, allow the silence to go on for a period of time, say 15 minutes. Beyond that, you might gently ask, "I'd like to check in with you. What's going on?" It may be that their inner experience is profoundly spiritual or hugely healing for them, and they may be able to let you know.

If it becomes clear that the journeyer is avoiding real work by dissociating, bring it to their attention and suggest some things to get them back into the room and back into their body. Deep, even breathing will generally bring them back, but it may not. You don't want to force them to do anything. You might try saying something like, "Be aware that you are dissociating. Don't beat yourself up about it, but when you catch yourself spacing out, gently bring your attention back into your body and breath." Or you might say, "I want you to get the most out of your session today. I wonder if this might be a good time to re-focus on your intentions." Sometimes, people need to dissociate for a while to let their nervous system calm down because they are on the cusp of some really scary work or are consciously or unconsciously overwhelmed. It's important for the sitter to honor this, but if it goes on more than 20 minutes, it is a waste of valuable session time.

Time is relative for the journeyer. In an altered state so much can be happening inside that ten minutes may seem like an hour, or an hour can seem like ten minutes.

Prior to the journey, the journeyer may identify certain areas of work or inquiry they wish to explore during the session. These areas may be promptly forgotten once the journey begins, and the first couple hours may be taken up with more urgent issues that have emerged. If there is a period later in the journey when the main work seems to be done and nothing new is coming up, the sitter may choose to remind the journeyer about one of those areas. Valuable exploration may be done when the person is still in an altered state.

Healing Comments

When people talk about "expanded awareness" in regard to psychedelics, they mean that these substances, when used properly, can let people see past the constrictions, absurdities, and fallacies of their prior social conditioning. The mind-expanding properties of psychedelics allow journeyers to be open and receptive to correcting erroneous, self-deprecating beliefs about themselves. Corrective, healing moments that would take years to open up in psychoanalysis or psychodynamic psychotherapy often occur in one or two sessions of psychedelic therapy. This is one of the things that makes psychedelics so powerful as a therapeutic tool.

In journeyspace, the journeyer's inner wisdom may focus their attention on certain strongly conditioned beliefs about themselves and others that do not reflect reality. For instance, as a result of early family and societal events, journeyers may believe they are inferior, incompetent, or downright worthless. They may believe no one will ever care what they think or what they need. As a result, when someone has listened to, respected and cared for them, they have not been able to take it in. In journeyspace, the person will be able to see and discard such self-destructive patterns of thought and feeling, realizing they arose out of damaging childhood events. A sitter's carefully placed, corrective comment at a critical moment can activate this insight.

For example, when a survivor of childhood abuse is feeling they were intrinsically bad and deserving of punishment, the sitter can help them re-frame this archaic belief by pointing out that it was the perpetrator who was bad. Simple, affirming statements like "Everything about you is good" can sink deeply into the unconscious mind at this time in the journey because the expanded mind is able to see that it could be true. You might repeat the statement several times to give the shift time to take place.

Another time is when someone in journeyspace is feeling the pain of their neglected inner child's core belief that he or she is unlovable. They can revise that belief with the help of true statements like "You were lovable, but your parents did not have the love you needed" or "There is nothing wrong with you. There was something wrong with your parents."

Another journeyer, who was neglected or abused as a child, may hold a deep belief that no one cares about their welfare. At the point in the session when they are feeling the pain of that belief, simple statements like "You matter" can help them let go of it.

When a journeyer is remembering childhood events where developmentally normal sexual curiosity and exploration were shamed, punished, or suppressed, a sitter can interject a supportive comment that normalizes and celebrates budding childhood sexuality.

If the journeyer is feeling hopeless at the emerging realization of how damaged they are, a simple and true statement like "There is much more to you than your damage" can put things in perspective.

Sometimes it's appropriate for the sitter to keep quiet and let the journeyer feel like a bad person. If the journeyer becomes aware that they acted without integrity or thoughtlessly hurt someone, allow time for them to be remorseful. If the sitter says anything, it might be "I believe you need to feel that."

Re-parenting

Sometimes journeyers may spontaneously age-regress. They become soft and vulnerable, like a little child. They may even act and talk in a child-like manner. When this happens, a nurturing bond with the sitter provides a rare opportunity to fulfill unmet or inadequately met early childhood developmental needs. Being held and comforted with tender, non-sexual touch and soothing, parental words of unconditional love is profoundly healing for adults who were emotionally neglected as children.

MDMA is especially effective at opening a window in time through which a caring sitter can re-parent a journeyer who felt unloved as a child. Those who were never securely attached or bonded with their mother may experience a deep, symbiotic melting when being cradled in the sitter's embrace. For some, this may be the first time they have ever let in love. Gentle back rubs, belly rubs, hugs, and foot massages are calming. Having a hand to hold helps in the scary moments. A teddy bear, baby bottle, and pacifier can be deeply soothing.

Those who were never held as children, or were never given safe, loving touch, may not know they need nurturing contact when distressed. The sitter may have to intuit their need for comfort and then initiate appropriate, tender touch.

Remember, you must always ask the journeyer permission before initiating any sort of physical contact. There should be a prior agreement that if the journeyer expresses discomfort, the contact will stop or change. You must be sure that your physical contact with the journeyer does not come from your own needs or desires.

A sitter's loving, parental gaze and voice tone that acknowledges the journeyer's suffering can be deeply healing. A sitter might say something like one of these: "That must have really hurt." "I'm so sad that happened to you. You didn't deserve that." "If I were your parent, I would never let anybody hurt you." In order to have deep impact, these words must come from a place of heartfelt empathy within the sitter.

Most psychological wounds can be traced back to a lack of love. Therefore, love is the ultimate healer.

If you are raised by wolves, you will act like a wolf. If are raised by parents who only validate the parts of you they like, you will create a false self to get their love and approval. If your parents only praise academic achievement, athletic ability, physical attractiveness, or monetary success, there may be vital parts of your authentic self that lie dormant. A sitter can observe and mirror back parts of the journeyer's natural self that may not have been seen or supported by their parents. Qualities such as goodness, sensitivity, intuition, depth, creativity, integrity, psychic ability, and an innate connection to spirit can be acknowledged and supported by the sitter.

Witness/Record Keeper

A sitter should be an attentive, attuned observer of everything that unfolds during a journey.

Keep a record of what takes place and when. Make note of medicines, dosages, and times taken. Note observable body language, energy shifts, releases, words spoken, discussions during the journey, and anything else that may seem important to report after the journey is over.

Sometimes the journeyer won't remember parts of the session. They may have exhibited significant body movements and activities that they were not aware of during the journey. As a witness, the sitter can document and report these observations. A review of notes after the journey can help jog the journeyer's memory of moments that deserve attention. Such information can help uncover patterns and promote insight.

In the days after a journey, some people find it valuable to review and process audio or video recordings of their session.

Deejay

Softly played background music can have a powerful effect in journeyspace. Appropriate music can help keep the mind quiet, promote relaxation, and evoke emotional responses.

Most music should be ambient, instrumental, and non-intrusive.

Soft chanting in foreign languages, Kirtan, and trance-inducing drumming are OK. Sometimes, more dynamic, emotionally evocative music may help the journeyer access deeper feeling states.

Musical options should be discussed before the session begins. Some journeyers will prefer quiet.

Even if the journeyer has requested quiet, it can be beneficial to introduce certain kinds of music at appropriate times. For instance, when repressed grief needs to be felt, sad music encourages deeper feeling. Conversely, if a journeyer is accessing primal strengths, upbeat music with drumming can encourage empowerment. But be careful: As deejay, the sitter should play music that supports or enhances the journeyer's unfolding experience rather than programming it.

Music should be carefully pre-screened to avoid anything remotely ominous or dark. Scary music can unnecessarily plunge a journeyer into a bleak place.

Music that works for one person might have no effect on another, or it might even be intolerable. A song that brought out a river of tears on one journey might be experienced on the same person's next journey as an irritation.

The sitter should always let it be known that music can be stopped or changed if it is not working for the journeyer.

Outside Contact

Sometimes, a journeyer may want to call, text, or go see someone right in the middle of a journey. This is never a good idea. Get them to wait until the journey is over. If they make a call, the journeyer is unlikely to remember what they said. They may scare or alienate the person they are calling, and there may be a lot of difficult explaining to do later. Don't let them do it.

If the journeyer wants to go outside during a journey, it may or may not be a good idea. If you have a private back yard, live in a natural setting, or have isolated nature nearby, this can be a healing environment for journeywork. If, however, the journeyer insists on going to a public area, or to visit a neighbor, talk them out of it! This activity is distracting, potentially dangerous, and is unlikely to result in any productive healing work.

Primitive Behavior

Journeyers are likely to engage in behavior that might be called primitive. There can be screaming, wailing, thrashing, belching, passing gas, throwing up, unleashing furious rage, animalistic behavior, taking clothes off, etc. It's important for the sitter to remain calm, accepting, and supportive. Know that deep wounds can find release and healing through these primitive behaviors. If you are freaked out by what you see, the journeyer will immediately pick up on your revulsion and think they are doing something wrong. Be prepared for primitive behavior to come up, and show acceptance when it does.

Magnified Transference

Transference is the unconscious, irrational transfer onto others of positive or negative feelings, expectations, or qualities that were originally associated with significant persons in one's past. Psychedelics like LSD and psilocybin can greatly amplify transference. The higher the dose, the greater the possibility that a journeyer's childhood relationship issues will be re-created in a transference onto the sitter. Within the safety of the therapeutic relationship, transference allows repressed memories of childhood relational dynamics to be brought to awareness and worked through.

For instance, in an altered state, journeyers may believe that the sitter is judging them, upset with them, or doesn't truly care about them. The sitter should encourage the sharing of these feelings and perceptions. If needed, the sitter may gently correct the journeyer's erroneous projections (e.g., by saying "I am not upset with you"). The sitter can then encourage the journeyer to look in their past for the origin of their assumptions.

For example, a journeyer believes that her expressions of deep emotional pain are being judged by the sitter. She imagines the sitter is thinking that she is acting or being dramatic. The sitter might respond with something like, "Your emotions feel very real to me, I'm sure you're not acting. Your feelings are big and important. When you were a child, I wonder who made you feel like you were being dramatic?"

During a journey, anger toward someone in the journeyer's past who hurt or abused them may be transferred onto the sitter. This is most likely to happen when the perpetrator was a parent or caregiver. On rare occasions, journeyers may scream angry accusations at the sitter. This is a challenge for even the most compassionate sitter. The sitter must stay calm, not get defensive, not retaliate, not take it personally, and not distance from the journeyer. The journeyer should be allowed to express anger as long as it is not physically abusive to the sitter or destructive to the environment.

People living with Dissociative Identity Disorder (multiple personalities) and Borderline Personality Disorder usually have angry, distrusting parts of themselves that may emerge and direct their hatred onto the sitter. Psychedelic work can be effective in treating Dissociative Identity Disorder, but it is NOT recommended for Borderline Personality Disorder.

Repressed memories can sometimes show up as transference hallucinations. Scenarios from the journeyer's past can be projected onto the sitter. For example, a woman is journeying with a male therapist. During the journey she regresses into a frightened little girl. Her body shakes, she curls up in fetal position and sucks her thumb. She looks at the sitter with frightened eyes. The sitter asks, "Are you afraid of me?" She replies, "Yes, you are looking at me sexually and playing with yourself." An objective part of her is aware that the sitter is not actually doing this, but this is what she is seeing and feeling. The sitter assures her this is untrue and encourages her to stay with the scary experience. When she is coming down from the drugs she processes the experience with the sitter. She begins to understand the transference as an important stage in uncovering and healing her early childhood sexual abuse.

In high-dose psychedelic therapy, the ideal is to have two sitters, one male and one female. This way, if the journeyer starts projecting negative transference onto one of the sitters and starts feeling unsafe, the other sitter can take over.

The sitter should NEVER role-play a perpetrator from the journeyer's past. Verbally or physically acting a role as a technique to trigger emotions or memories of past trauma is dangerous. In an altered state, the journeyer may lose the ability to tell the difference between the perpetrator in the past and the present person of the sitter. When this happens, the journeyer will feel completely unsafe and will be re-traumatized.

Patience

Being a sitter requires patience. You will be devoting six to eight hours (occasionally more) to being present and attentive to the journeyer. You may need to listen, be attuned and responsive to hours of verbal processing. There may be hours of intense emotional catharsis and somatic releasing. There may be repetitive ranting in which the same phrases or expletives are repeated over and over again for hours.

There may be hours of silence when journeyers are deeply engrossed in internal experiences. When it appears that nothing important is happening, you will need patience, wisdom, and restraint not to interfere prematurely or inappropriately to make something happen. Although these times can be tedious for the sitter, your presence is crucial for the important work that is going on inside the journeyer.

Psychedelically-assisted psychotherapy is an extremely accelerated modality. Many people's lives improve markedly from a single session. However, some wounds still take a long time to heal. If you are working with those who have known enormous or prolonged trauma, you will need to be patient and supportive for healing processes that may take years to complete. Also, certain therapies may take quite a few journeys just to get off the ground. Here are some things you may face:

• It may take a few sessions for a neophyte journeyer to feel safe being open and vulnerable in altered states, even when the medicine is MDMA.

• Working with those who have early childhood attachment and bonding wounds may require many journeys devoted to building a foundation of connection and trust within the therapeutic relationship.

- Initial journeys need to be gentle, positive experiences. You must establish a basic infrastructure of strength before delving into traumatic material.

- You may need to work slowly through psychological defenses before it is possible to access and heal core issues.

Rigid individuals who need to stay in control will have the most difficulty letting go into an altered state. They may unconsciously fight the drug for the entire journey. These highly defended people seldom experience the full effect of the drug. They may experience intense anxiety and/or a variety of unpleasant psychosomatic symptoms.

When journeyers are resistant to treatment and are not getting results, a frustrated sitter should NEVER blame the journeyer. Never make comments like, "You aren't trying hard enough." There are always painful origins for strong defenses. Be patient and compassionate.

Being a sitter is exciting, fascinating, sacred work but it's often draining, sometimes tedious, and occasionally boring.

Spiritual Support

An ideal sitter must be able to support, understand, and validate any spiritual experiences and epiphanies that emerge in journeywork. It's essential for the sitter to work within the journeyer's personal spiritual or religious paradigms. To validate the journeyer's experience, it may occasionally help if the sitter shares personal spiritual experiences, wisdom, or beliefs. The sitter should clearly state that these are personal experiences and beliefs, not absolute truths. It is never appropriate for the sitter to impose their beliefs on the journeyer.

Silence is Golden

A sitter should always refrain from excessive talking. In an altered state, the journeyer is often too deep inside themself to engage in a real dialogue, and too high to follow complex conversation. Journeyers are highly suggestible and vulnerable, so be very careful what you say. Do not preach, analyze, interpret, or engage in intellectual discourse. Keep comments short. Speak in simple language. A judicious amount of guidance and support from an experienced sitter can be important, but when in doubt, don't say anything.

The Sitter's Pre-journey Briefing

It's a good idea for the sitter to communicate rules and guidelines before the start of a first session with a new journeyer. This can eliminate unnecessary confusion, fears, concerns, and ambiguities during the journey.

The following is a sample directive used by the author:

1. There is no right way to do journeys. Everyone is different; every journey is different. You can experiment with going deeper by closing your eyes, breathing, and focusing on your inner world.

2. You may get deep insights and clarity during the journey, but the most profound healing and transformation often happens beyond

words or thinking. Thus, results may not become evident until the days or weeks following the journey.

3. I (the sitter) do not have a universal treatment plan that I will impose on your experience. I believe each person has their own, unique healing path, inner wisdom, and guidance. I will support that.

4. If I am being too directive or talking too much, it's important that you let me know. Conversely, if I am silent, and you need guidance or help, let me know that.

5. If I say or do something that annoys you, pisses you off, or makes you feel unsafe, it is VERY important to let me know. My feelings will not be hurt. If you hold your feelings in, we could miss some important issue that needs to be explored. Unspoken discord between us can seriously compromise the success of the journey.

6. I am very interested in hearing about your unfolding journey experience, but there is no need to report everything to me. If a lot is happening internally, stopping to talk about it can remove you from the experience. It's like being on a roller coaster while trying to have a conversation with your ride partner. If there is something important you want to share or make sure you'll remember later, tell me and I will write it down. We can always talk about your experience after the session.

7. The only directive I may be somewhat relentless about is making sure you are aware of your breath and fully breathing. Focusing

on your breath helps keep your chattering mind quiet by giving it something simple and hypnotic to focus on. Breathing helps relax chronic constrictions, allowing emotions and traumatic memories to surface and release. Breathing keeps the healing process moving.

8. Make sure to let me know if you need a drink of water or are uncomfortable, too cold or hot. I have blankets, fans, etc., to insure your comfort.

9. You may choose to have silence or some appropriate, non-intrusive journey music to help you relax. If you have opted for music, but it's not working for you, let me know so I can change it or turn it off. If you have chosen silence, I may, at my discretion, put on some music I think might help you get deeper into an emerging feeling. For example, if you need to feel deeper into some grief or pain, I may put on sad music to help elicit tears. If the music is not right, let me know.

10. There are boundaries on appropriate behavior within your session.

Touch: If you need a hand to hold or some other comforting touch, ask for it. I will never touch you without first asking if you are OK with it. If you become uncomfortable with our contact at any time let me know and I will stop.

Sex: It's OK to honor and work with sexual feelings and material that comes up, but there will NEVER be anything sexual allowed between us.

Anger: This is a safe place to release repressed anger. I'm comfortable with it and encourage it. It's OK to scream as loud as you want, and I have a punching bag, etc., if needed. My boundaries are that you are not allowed to harm me or damage my stuff.

11. Sitter's needs:

I will need to go to the bathroom now and then.

I will need to eat something at some point during the journey.

I may need to stand and stretch occasionally.

I will be with you the entire journey unless you need private space. If you need time alone I will stay within earshot. Let me know when you want me back.

12. Everything that happens and is said here will remain confidential.

13. If you are taking a high dose of psilocybin, at some point in the journey you may believe you are going crazy or dying. It may feel very real and frightening. I assure you that this is a safe, transformational process that will wind down as the drug wears off.

7. GUIDELINES FOR THE PROFESSIONAL PSYCHOTHERAPIST

If a patient of yours has expressed an interest in using psychedelics for emotional healing, you will want to know about safety and efficacy. Many of your questions can be addressed by learning about the numerous government-approved studies undertaken in the past few years. The best resource for this is the Multidisciplinary Association for Psychedelic Studies website (www.MAPS.org).

Regarding safety, two questions are paramount. First, is it physically safe for your patient to ingest LSD, psilocybin (mushrooms), and/or MDMA (ecstasy)? Research conforming to modern drug-development standards has been conducted regarding the safety of each of these substances in its pure form. None has been shown to have lasting toxicity. In practice, responsible psychedelic users take into account that LSD and MDMA have stimulant effects. Although there are no reported cases of injury from using these substances in journeys, caution makes psilocybin the best choice for journeyers who have high blood pressure or other heart-related conditions.

Second, as a result of things that have happened when unstable people used psychedelics recreationally, some wonder whether these drugs can ever be psychiatrically safe. When practiced using the guidelines in this manual, psychedelic therapy is safe for normally functioning people. Psychedelic substances do their work by allowing people to bypass their usual defenses. Some people are already too open and uncontained to live a stable life. Psychedelic therapy would do them no good, and might impair their already shaky functioning.

With rare exceptions, the following people should not use psychedelics, even in a controlled therapeutic setting:

1. Those who have been diagnosed as having a personality disorder.

2. Those who have had manic or major depressive episodes significant enough to impair functioning or cause hospitalization.

3. Those who have periods of being actively suicidal, or who cut themselves or engage in similar self-harming behavior.

4. Those who have schizophrenic or other psychotic disorders.

5. Those with severely impaired impulse control.

6. Survivors of satanic ritual abuse.

Psychedelic psychotherapy is an excellent treatment for adults who are so defended against or troubled by past trauma that they now suffer from anxiety, depression, and an inability to form satisfying relationships. We know this as Post-traumatic Stress Disorder. Typically, it results from childhood physical, sexual or emotional abuse; rape; catastrophic accident or injury; and war.

There are two things psychedelic therapy can offer, when it is used as an adjunct to psychoanalysis or psychotherapy, which likely will not be achieved through more conventional means. Its most gratifying effect occurs when a patient is truly stuck, unable to move forward in treatment or in life. One to three sessions of psychedelic therapy can safely expose buried feelings and memories to the light of day, where they can be processed and released or integrated during the session, or in the patient's regular therapy once the door has been opened.

Sometimes clients who are not completely stuck just don't have the perseverance for conventional psychotherapy. Such a person may see psychedelic work as a way to speed up the healing process. This is accurate; it will. Applying psychedelic therapy at judicious intervals during the person's work with you will ensure that the healing moves along at a good clip.

Psychedelic therapy may occasionally expose repressed material faster than it can be adequately processed. Stay alert for signs that your client is becoming less stable. Point out these signs firmly, talk about the possible consequences of continuing, and ask your client to halt the psychedelic sessions until he or she has been able to integrate everything that has been unearthed so far.

What if you want to do psychedelic psychotherapy with your own clients?

Although a therapist's sensibilities are helpful in any kind of healing work, there is little resemblance between the job of a professional psychotherapist and that of a sitter. The principal psychotherapist in psychedelic psychotherapy is the client's inner wisdom. Trained psychotherapists find it difficult to stay silent and not try to help, but in a journey, therapeutic interventions can often interfere with an inwardly-guided process that is already well underway.

You know that a psychotherapist, to be any good, must go through his or her own therapy first. Similarly, your client deserves a sitter who is personally familiar with psychedelic work. The way to understand what is and is not needed in a journey is to have been a journeyer yourself numerous times, assisted by an experienced sitter. Only in that way will you attain a sense of what is and is not constructive in the work of a sitter.

8. PREPARATION FOR THE JOURNEY

A setting which both protects and supports the work is essential to a journey's success. The most important things to organize in advance are sound considerations, appearance, comfort, and the arrangement of the physical space.

Journey space must allow for noisy, cathartic venting because some people need to scream out their pain and rage during journeys. Often there is little or no warning. They might yell, wail, scream out obscenities, and make all kinds of animalistic, primitive sounds. Some people may have ten completely quiet, inward journeys, but on the eleventh they may go bonkers! Be prepared.

A soundproof room would be ideal. Lacking that, if you have close neighbors, you would be well advised to prepare them. Let them know you will be having therapy (or acting class, or whatever) that could involve making loud noise, so they don't worry if they hear yelling or crying. This way you will not get a visit from the police or be interrupted by freaked-out neighbors concerned for your safety. If circumstances require you to keep things quiet, screaming into a pillow will muffle most of the sound.

To the extent that you can, protect the journeyspace from the distraction of abrupt outside noise. For instance, on the day of the journey, don't schedule someone to repair the plumbing or use a chain saw to prune a tree on the property. If your next door neighbor is having a party, just close the windows. It will be fine as long as the journeyer knows the context for human noise. It may even bring up memories that move the journey forward.

A journey room should be a cozy, pleasant, private space. A journeyer who becomes stuck in fear should be able to open their eyes and see things that support them to calm down and feel safe. An ideal journey room should have soft, soothing colors and fabrics, reassuring art and art objects, empowering religious or spiritual symbols, living plants, and gentle lighting.

The space should allow the journeyer to move about, dance, do yoga, etc. It should have a comfortable area for reclining and relaxing; and it should be flexible. During parts of a session, the journeyer may want you to be very close. At other times, they may want you farther away or behind a barrier of pillows.

Some people roll or thrash around during journeywork. As much as possible, the space where the journeyer will be working should be softly padded. A king or queen size mattress on a carpeted floor is ideal. Gym mats, floor pads, and assorted sized pillows may come in handy. Sharp objects, hard furniture with sharp edges, and breakable items should be kept away from the immediate journey space.

Things You Will Need on the Journey

Basics:

• The journeyer should wear comfortable, loose-fitting clothing. They should dress in layers to accommodate fluctuations of body temperature during the session. For the same reason, equip the room with extra sheets and blankets.

• To support the journey, there should be audio equipment for the sitter to play soft, non-intrusive instrumental or emotive music. Journeyers may bring their own personal music that evokes feelings or memories.

• Fan and/or heater.

• Water (in unbreakable bottles).

• Kleenex.

• A large bowl in case the journeyer needs to throw up. Use an unbreakable bowl with a flat bottom that won't tip over easily. Two bowls are good. If the journeyer vomits into one bowl, you can replace it with a fresh, empty one without having to leave the journey room.

• A towel or two.

• A sleep mask or eye pillow to cover the eyes.

• A punching bag or a firm, heavy pillow to hit.

Optional:

• Journeyers may bring childhood photos of themselves at different ages, plus photos of parents, siblings, and other significant persons.

- Recording device (audio or video).
- A favorite stuffed animal.
- Toys, dolls, puppets, etc. (for play therapy if journeyer is regressed).
- Drawing materials (crayons and a big sketch pad work well).
- Baby pacifier and baby bottle (for regressed states).
- Heating pad (soothing for hurting places on journeyer's body).
- Disposable, absorbent bed pads and/or adult diapers. (On rare occasions someone may have childhood toilet training issues or fears of letting go of bowel control during a journey. Having these on hand allows the journeyer and sitter to relax and not worry about this issue.)
- A rubber dog bone or something similar to bite down on (for primal anger work).
- Sacred objects or objects personally significant to the journeyer.

A journey takes six to eight hours. The journeyer should set aside the rest of that day for recovery and integration. This time must be free from all commitments and obligations. On the day of the journey, it's essential there be no interruptions from visitors, delivery or service people, and the like. Turn off all phones during the time of the journey.

If the journey takes place away from the journeyer's home, they should arrange to have a friend drive them and pick them up. Even if they think they will be OK to drive after the journey, not having to worry about being sober enough to drive can help them relax more deeply into altered states during the journey.

At least one day after the session should be reserved to rest and process the journey experience. This is best done alone. If there can be two or three days' down time after the journey, all the better.

9. GUIDELINES FOR THE JOURNEYER

Getting Started

Avoid scary, violent media, and upsetting situations the day before your journey, if possible. Whatever you put into your consciousness may show up in your journey experience.

Get a good night's sleep the night before a journey, if possible. Conscious and unconscious anxiety about the journey may make sleep difficult. You might consider taking a moderate dose of Valium, melatonin or some herbal sleep formula to help. Expect to be anxious. You are heading into the unknown. The unknown is always scary. Anxiety may make you feel nauseous or sick. Even seasoned journeyers often experience anxiety before each new journey.

Don't eat at least four hours prior to your journey. You will not feel hungry once the journey starts. Do not eat until after the session. If you are hypoglycemic, a three-hour fast will be adequate if your last meal is light (no meat). Eating too close to the time you take psychedelics will DRASTICALLY reduce the effect of the drugs, and may cause nausea. Prepare a meal that will be ready to eat after the journey.

Wear comfortable, loose-fitting clothing.

Turn off all phones. Make sure all obligations, including pets and children, will be someone else's responsibility for the duration of your journey, and for some time thereafter.

Bring your sitter up to date about any important new developments in your life that have not been previously discussed. Make sure to clear any fears or issues about going into journeyspace.

Say a prayer and/or state your intentions. Your intention may be to address specific issues, or to simply trust the wisdom and guidance of a Higher Power.

Take your planned medications, lie down or sit comfortably, and start breathing.

Everyone will have different journey experiences. No two journeys for any one person will ever be alike either. So, the first hard and fast rule is that there are no hard and fast rules about how to journey.

Coming On

"Whenever there is a reaching down into innermost experience, into the nucleus of personality, most people are overcome by fright, and run away.... The risk of inner experience, the adventure of the spirit, is in any case, alien to most human beings." ~ Carl Jung, Memories, Dreams, Reflections

If you have never taken psychedelics before or have had a bad experience with them in the past, approaching your psychedelic therapy session may be scary. The transition from a normal waking state to an altered state may be fraught with conscious or unconscious anxiety.

It generally takes 45 minutes to an hour for most meds to start working. As you begin coming on, you'll probably feel anxious. Your heart rate may increase. You may tremble, tingle, become nauseous, hot, or chilled. If you feel the urge to vomit, try to keep it down for the first hour so you don't throw up the medicine. You may experience an alarming rush of fear when the drug begins to take effect. Don't panic. This will pass as you begin to feel safe and comfortable being in an altered state.

To encourage the deepest possible passage into journeyspace, lie down, get cozy, and restrict extraneous talking. Close your eyes, if you are comfortable doing so. Begin quieting your mind by focusing on your breath. Yoga, stretching, or dance movement may help focus your attention out of your thoughts and into your body. Soft, meditative, instrumental music may help you relax.

After coming on, the potency of the meds will build for the next hour or so. You will then have about three to four hours of prime working time before the drug starts winding down.

Letting Go of Control

"Man cannot discover new oceans unless he has the courage to lose sight of the shore." ~ Andre Gide

Psychedelics are powerful keys that can unlock the natural healing intelligence within you. Psychedelic therapy works best when you can step out of the way and allow the healing to occur. The best approach is to set intentions about what issues need healing, then let go of expectations and ideas about how to fix these issues. Trust a deeper intelligence. The more you journey, the more you will come to trust this inner guidance.

The idea of being under the influence of a mind-altering drug may seem dangerous. You may fear the drug will be in control, not you. If you are not in control, you may be afraid of experiencing something scary that you will not be able to handle. You may fear you will act in a way that will be embarrassing or destructive. You may be afraid of revealing parts of yourself that are hidden or repressed. You may fear being too honest, open, and vulnerable. You may be afraid that you'll become addicted, permanently incapacitated, go crazy, or die. Rest assured, you will be able to relinquish control incrementally, at your own pace.

If letting go into a deeper experience becomes scary, reassuring words and nurturing contact from your sitter may help. Guided meditations and peaceful music may also promote letting go. If you are feeling overwhelmed, you can keep your eyes open and pay attention to something pleasurable. Letting go into an altered state feels like falling asleep to some people. Rest assured that your sitter will awaken you if you do fall asleep.

With practice, you will begin to trust that you have control if things get scary. Moderate doses of psychedelics can be willfully controlled. If you are afraid of encountering inner demons, know that your psyche will present to awareness only as much difficult material as you can presently handle. Beyond that point you will usually space out, get distracted, or become sober.

Staying Out of Your Head

Your intellect is an amazing computer. Give it a task and it can do marvelous things. Left to run on its own, it can drive you crazy.

The best advice for getting the most out of a journey is to stay out of your incessantly chattering mind. The first step towards getting out of your head is to realize that you are in it! In journeyspace you may become acutely aware of how thinking distracts you from deeper experiences. Unless you are an accomplished meditator, holding your attention beyond your thoughts will be a challenge.

To discipline a scattered mind you must focus your attention like a laser beam. Concentration on the rhythmic rising and falling of your chest and belly directs awareness out of your head and into your body. Deep breathing also softens chronic muscle tension and lowers anxiety, allowing access to blocked emotions and the body's own healing wisdom.

In the course of a journey you may experience waves of exciting insight. Familiar ideas may suddenly be understood in startling new ways. Psychological concepts you've understood intellectually may suddenly be felt experientially. You may receive fresh perspectives and revelations about issues, situations, and problems you have been grappling with for years. Profound realizations may pop up out of the blue. This whirlwind of new information is exhilarating to the intellect. A rush of thoughts can keep your attention engrossed in your head. Your mind may delight in pondering the significance of all this titillating new information. In journeyspace it is usually difficult to follow lengthy trains of thought, but it is still possible to get lost in your head for long periods of time.

Every time you stop to analyze your experience during a journey, you interrupt the ongoing experience. Analyzing is different than insight. Analysis is a directed, time-consuming process that uses the left brain to understand something. Insight that emerges in journeyspace is a spontaneous "Aha!" phenomenon. It's like a light bulb switched on in a darkened room. You may want to make an audio recording of your journey so important insights can be verbalized and recorded as they occur. This way, you are free to stay present during the journey, knowing you can remember and reflect upon insights later, when the recording is played back.

If you were traumatized as a bright child, you may have escaped into your head to avoid feeling the neglect or abuse you endured. You may have become a bookworm or an A student. As an adult, you may ruminate as a way to avoid painful feelings. You may have split off from your embodied, emotional self, into the safe world of your mind.

When this happens, your mind can become a tyrannical devil with a will of its own. Its mission is to perpetually distract you from painful memories and feelings--regardless of the cost. Your mind will convince you that letting go of its protective control is dangerous.

Encountering Defenses

If you feel sober, restless, hungry, chatty, or sleepy, you are probably encountering defenses. If you feel compelled to flee or order pizza, recognize these impulses as resistance.

There are many forms of resistive behavior. The most common is the unwillingness or inability to stay out of your head. Exciting thoughts, insights, and fantasies can distract you from deeper growth and healing.

Another common form of resistance is the unwillingness or inability to stay focused on intent. You may drift off into daydreams or feel compelled to engage in diversionary activities or thoughts in order to avoid dealing with more uncomfortable situations, issues and feelings.

Spiritually oriented people may habitually resist exploration of their body and negative emotions. They may prefer to float in a state of transcendent bliss. This can be a valid, transformational experience for some, but a form of avoidance and escape for others.

Some degree of resistance is normal for everyone. It may last only a short time and dissipate without much effort.

Overcoming Defenses

You will need sincere commitment and discipline to get through persistent defenses.

The most universally effective way to soften resistance is to breathe deeply and continuously. Full, unimpeded breathing means both the chest and abdomen rise and fall with each inhale and exhale in a gentle, rhythmic sequence. During inhalation the abdomen begins to swell slightly before the chest expands. Effort is concentrated on inflating the belly and the chest. During exhalation the chest begins to deflate before the abdomen. The breath is released effortlessly, not pushed out with force.

If you are a shallow breather, you may find deep breathing difficult or even painful at first. Shallow breathing is a common defense mechanism that can minimize bad feelings. If you grew up in an unsafe environment, your diaphragm and rib cage may be chronically "frozen in fear." You may have learned to hold your breath to stop unwanted feelings. Deep breathing reverses this process. It unlocks the rib cage and diaphragm. It allows you to move through defenses and feel emotions.

To move beyond anxious defenses, try focusing your attention inside your body to find where you feel the fear. You may discover jittery sensations or tightness in your belly, for example. With each inhalation, imagine that you are sending peace and healing into the frightened areas. Imagine releasing the fear with each exhalation.

Breathing deeply into places in your body where you hold fear promotes calm, and induces the discharge of trauma that may be stored there.

There are other ways to soften defenses. Ask your sitter for comforting physical contact that feels safe and calming (like holding hands or being held). Hug a teddy bear. Visualize yourself in a peaceful setting in your mind's eye. For example, you could imagine yourself romping through soft grasses in a spring meadow, or lounging on a secluded, tropical beach. This can be a familiar place you've been or a fantasy you make up. Immerse all your senses in this experience. Imagine feeling the warm sand under your feet, smell the ocean breeze, etc. If you believe in a higher power, call on the presence of that power for protection and comfort.

Do not criticize or belittle yourself for being fearful. Underneath our tough adult armor we are all scared little children. A man who is fearless on the battlefields of war and business may be terrified to be soft and vulnerable.

Appreciate that your defenses have been vital, protective mechanisms that allowed you to survive trauma. Psychological defenses may be the cornerstones that have supported your internal status quo. Your very survival may feel threatened by disturbing this status quo. In the face of overwhelming trauma, defenses act like internal circuit-breakers that protect the fragile psyche. Dismantling defenses may feel like re-exposing yourself to the terror of certain annihilation.

To illustrate this concept, imagine you are a two year-old child playing at the seashore. A storm begins to generate terrifying, six foot waves that could easily drown you. To protect yourself, you build a six foot-high wall between you and the menacing surf. As years go by, you grow stronger and taller. The wall has successfully protected you from being drowned. Today you are nearly a six foot-tall adult who can swim, yet you have never dared dismantle the wall. Inside you are still a vulnerable little two-year old who is terrified of six-foot waves. To unblock resistance, it's often helpful to remind your frightened inner child that you now have the strength, wits and resources to survive six-foot waves.

The experience of wrestling defenses is not limited to the beginning of journeys. Defenses will arise whenever you approach scary new issues, traumatic memories, or uncomfortable situations.

The amount and intensity of resistance is often directly proportionate to the amount and intensity of that which is resisted. You will strongly resist dealing with that which is most traumatic or uncomfortable to deal with. The greater the trauma, the stronger the defenses. If you encounter strong defenses, know that you are getting very close to something traumatic that is ready to be healed.

To move through stubborn defenses you may need to change

or augment the medicines you are using. So, for example, you encounter strong defenses during a journey in which you have not already taken the maximum dose of MDMA (about 200 mg). Taking additional MDMA at this stuck point may move you through defenses. An additional 50 to 75 mg may be sufficient. It's a good idea for the sitter to have these smaller doses prepared in advance for such emergencies. If you are working with LSD or psilocybin, you may need to increase the dosage of these meds to get beyond defenses.

If you are not able to break through resistance, just be aware that you are confronting your own defenses. You may have intellectual knowledge of psychological defenses, but never consciously experienced them in action. Awareness of when and how you unconsciously avoid scary feelings can be an important insight and the beginning of change.

Working through strong defenses may take time. You can't force it. Attempts to blast through defenses before you are ready will result in re-traumatizing. Learn to work gently, honoring your psyche's own wisdom and pace.

10. RESTORING SANITY WITH THE PEAK EXPERIENCE

Traditional psychotherapy and psychoanalysis concentrates on exploring what Carl Jung called the "shadow." The shadow is the unconscious part of ourselves we deny or repress. Parts of our shadow may contain painful, frightening thoughts, feelings, and sensations, and disturbing memories of childhood trauma that create problems for us as adults. Traditional therapy attempts to bring this unconscious material into conscious awareness so it can be dealt with.

Psychological healing with psychedelic drugs involves not only this shadow work, but also includes what is called the "peak experience." The peak experience is a sampling of how we might feel and perceive life if we had never been programmed or traumatized. It's an experience of peace, relaxation, and connection with Spirit. It is a fresh, "here and now" experience of the joy of existing without the fears, anxiety, neuroses, judgments, and conceptualizations that habitually contaminate our perception of reality. Words cannot adequately describe the places you may visit in non-ordinary states of consciousness. They are sacred experiences of sanity that can be remembered and used as reference points to cultivate and learn to reproduce without the drug as we heal and evolve.

The peak experience may be likened to rare days in Los Angeles, when strong winds clear out the smog. During this time you can see mountains and trees you never knew were there. Most of us have grown accustomed to living in a stressful, alienating, toxic fog for so long we are unaware of how dangerously out of balance, tense, and crazy we have become.

The beauty of psychoactive drugs is that within an hour or two, you can be lifted high above the fog into an experience of profound peace and sanity. Having such a peak experience can deeply enrich, balance, and transform your life.

Being

"How narrow is the vision that exalts the business of the ant above the singing of the grasshopper." ~ Kahlil Gibran

A basic element of peak experiences is the experience of "beingness." Beingness is a state of being spontaneous, uninhibited, and fully present in the moment. It's an experience of being fully aware of what's going on inside and outside your body. It requires a willingness to let go of control, personal agenda, and judgment in order to "go with the flow" of naturally unfolding events. It requires having a mind quiet enough to experience the exquisiteness of the ordinary.

Beingness is a natural, timeless state of simple existence that is shared by every species of life on the planet except adult human beings. The pace and complexity of modern culture has turned most human beings into "human doings." We are obsessed with achieving and consuming. We are driven by fear and desire. We are committed to the belief that life is a struggle and a puzzle to be figured out. We are so focused on securing the pot of gold, we miss the rainbow.

Beingness comes naturally to animals. Humans have great difficulty with it. Throughout history, mystics have dedicated their lives to meditation and the practice of austerities in order to experience pure states of beingness. What makes the achievement of these states so difficult is our human mind. Our thoughts cloud and distort our direct experience of life. Thinking keeps us constantly absorbed in the past and the future. To experience the present moment fully, we must gain control over the incessant chatter of our thoughts. Psychedelics can temporarily quiet the mind and induce states of beingness that are similar to those states that meditators spend years to achieve.

Seeing

"The real voyage of discovery consists not in seeking new landscapes, but in having new eyes." ~ Marcel Proust

Another element of the peak experience is "seeing." Seeing, in this context, is the experience of perceiving things as they are, without conceptualizing, categorizing, projecting, or judging. It's the ability to suspend the clatter of the analytical mind long enough to behold things afresh, with the eyes of a child.

As we become adults, most of us lose the ability to really see things. We become jaded. We no longer experience a tree as we did for the first time. Our eyes notice something green and tall, and our brain instantly identifies this object as a tree. We no longer behold the awesome phenomenon of a tree; we experience the abstract concept of a tree.

People live in a world of concepts, words, and pictures in their head that is removed from the direct, sensory experience of reality. Our nervous system and brain are bombarded with billions of bits of sense data every second. To protect ourselves from being overwhelmed and confused, our brains automatically ignore most everything that is not relevant for our immediate need, interest, or survival. Psychoactive drugs can temporarily override this reductive function. When our full range of awareness is restored, we can behold the beauty and magic of the world we live in.

"To be shaken out of the ruts of ordinary perception, to be shown for a few timeless hours the outer and the inner world, not as they appear to an animal obsessed with words and notions, but as they are apprehended, directly and unconditionally, by Mind at Large..." ~ Aldous Huxley, The Doors of Perception.

Knowing

"I did not arrive at my understanding of the fundamental laws of the universe with my rational mind." ~ Albert Einstein

Another element of the peak experience is a sense of instinctive, intuitive knowing. This non-rational knowledge supports inspired insight and inner guidance. During a peak experience, it's common to get fresh insights and see possible new solutions to problematic situations and relationships in your life. A journeyer can get clarity and a cosmic perspective on the overall direction and meaning of their life, and the meaning of life in general.

Being in an altered state enables a shift from a survival-oriented, intellect-dominated state into a more relaxed, expansive state. In this receptive state a journeyer experiences heightened awareness of subtle messages of instinct, intuition, and wisdom from their Higher Self.

There are many ways that psychoactive drugs encourage mind expansion. Psychoactive chemicals permit access to less dominant parts of the brain and encourage neurons to make fresh new connections.

Insight may also come when psychoactive drugs wake us from our enculturated trance. Most of us unknowingly live in a trance state of consensus reality that is the result of lifelong programming by our family, culture, and mass media. An infant born to a remote tribe in the Amazon jungle will grow up with a greatly different world view and experience of reality than an infant born in New York City.

Having a concrete experience of an alternative reality offers an expanded perspective from which we can see how our culture's mindset colors our thoughts, feelings, and perceptions. We may see clearly how our lives have been controlled by Madison Avenue, government propaganda, religious dogma, and social ethic. As we awaken from this trance, we begin to see the arbitrariness of social mores that have imprisoned us. This may open up an unlimited range of creative lifestyle options and new possibilities we may have never considered or dared to implement. We may also begin to appreciate the humor of it all. When people first begin using psychoactive drugs they often experience fits of uncontrollable laughter as they are struck with the absurdity of modern life.

Profound insight may also come from the shift of identification from the ego self to the authentic self. Most people assume that who they are is a composite of their body, thoughts, occupation, lifestyle, nationality, race, religion, political persuasion, favorite football team, and so on. Psychoactive drugs like LSD and psilocybin can break this trance, offering an experience of one's essence.

This essence is the "witness" that has been observing the world through your eyes and listening behind your ears since you were a baby. It has witnessed your body growing up. It will witness your body growing old. It witnesses your thoughts, your emotions, your pleasure, your pain, your successes, and your failures. It's constant, unchangeable, and indestructible. It is pure consciousness that outlives your body. Religions call it the Soul. Hindus call it Brahman, and describe it as: *"The imperishable, the supreme, dwelling in each body....Weapons cut it not; fire burns it not; water wets it not; wind dries it not."* ~ Bhagavad Gita 2:23

As you shift your identification from your ego self to your essence, you become lighter, freer, and less fearful. You gain access to the resources and wisdom of your Higher Self. You arrive at a dispassionate vantage point from which you can clearly observe your ego self and its pathology. You can monitor and examine your own thoughts, feelings, perceptions, and responses almost as if you were an objective outside observer. You begin to see the overall pattern and bigger picture of your life as if you were an eagle soaring high above your limited ego perspective.

Loving

"This is my commandment, that ye love one another, as I have loved you." ~ Jesus (John 13:34)

A common attribute of peak psychedelic experiences is a softening of emotional defenses and an engulfment in warm feelings that radiate from your own heart center.

Many of us in this culture walk around unconsciously protecting ourselves with thick walls of emotional armor. We've been forging and thickening these walls of steel since childhood. As infants and children, we instinctively reach out for love and seek physical and emotional intimacy. If we are ignored, rejected, or abused, we learn to surround our tender hearts with walls. We come to believe that no one can be trusted to enter. The same walls that protect us from being hurt again also hold us prisoner. Nothing and nobody can truly touch our hearts, and we can no longer reach out beyond the walls. As the years go by, we get so used to the walls that we forget we are in prison.

Under the influence of MDMA and other psychedelics, these walls begin to melt. Barriers of fear, judgment, and pretense that separate us from others begin to drop.

You may begin to feel a deep kinship, compassion, and unconditional love for all living beings. You may be filled with love and appreciation for those who are dear to you. You may experience a sense of well-being that promotes honest and open communication. You may feel uninhibited about being physically affectionate and close with friends and lovers. If your heart has been closed, you may experience letting love in for the first time in your adult life.

If you have been imprisoned for decades inside your own emotional walls, this ecstatic experience of love and openness offers an opportunity to feel connected in love to all humankind. This pleasurable experience may give you the awareness, motivation, and courage to begin the process of fashioning permanent doors and windows in your walls.

A forty year old first-time journeyer described her peak experience during her MDMA session:

"It's amazing to just feel relaxed, present, and comfortable in my own skin. No fear, no self-consciousness! I'm not monitoring everything I say. It's so different than how I always am. I've been so wound tight! I multi-task and schedule every minute of my life. Now I realize how much anxiety I usually feel. My legs and feet are trembling. How interesting! I'm letting my body do things I'm not in control of. I'm just letting my body BE. I don't have to analyze or DO anything. I'm learning how to just BE."

Limitations of the Peak Experience

Peak experiences can be powerfully eye-opening and transformational. Even so, positive results from peak experiences may be modest or fade in time if there are hidden or unhealed parts of the self that still need to be addressed.

Psychedelically induced spiritual awakenings can artificially bypass years of the earnest spiritual practice needed to cultivate lasting transformation. Without further integration of new awareness and insight experienced on these drugs, old habits and neuroses can soon return.

People who use psychoactive drugs recreationally often get depressed when the drug's effects wear off and they return to their mundane lives. Without doing rigorous inner work and making needed life changes, the recreational user may become dependent on the drug to access states of bliss. Some become addicted to the peak experience as an escape.

Using psychoactive drugs in this addictive way usually doesn't last long. At some point, during some journey, the unhealed parts of one's psyche eventually surface and plummet the user into a "bad trip." This unpleasant experience often discourages further recreational use. Others may eventually reach an unconscious barrier that shields unhealed parts of the psyche from awareness. When this happens, further levels of consciousness expansion and exploration are blocked, the peak experience is flattened, and the user soon loses interest in psychedelics.

11. EMBRACING THE SHADOW

There is a story about a holy man in India who spent many years meditating in a cave. He had reached a state of great peace and enlightenment through his simple life style and dedication to truth.

One day, the holy man went out to gather wood for a fire. When he returned to his cave he found terrifying, saucer-eyed demons in it! He dropped his wood and ran away, hoping the demons would leave on their own accord. The next day he returned to his cave. The demons were still there. The holy man decided to sit nearby to meditate and pray for God to take the demons away. He sat deeply meditating and praying all day and all night. In the morning the demons were still there. He became furious. He gathered up his courage, stormed up to his cave, and screamed at the demons. He threw rocks at them and commanded them to leave. The demons did not budge. The man gave up. That night, in his sleep, he received an inspiration. The next morning he went into his cave and prepared tea for the demons. He sat and talked with them all day and all night. The following day the demons left amicably and never returned.

To banish your demons, you must be willing to delve beyond peak experiences to explore hidden, scary parts of your shadow. The shadow self contains the parts that you unconsciously conceal from yourself and others. Your shadow may contain shameful, frightening, painful thoughts, feelings, impulses, and memories you do not want to see or feel. These are your demons. The only way to make them leave is to invite them to tea and conversation.

You cannot captain your own ship as long as you are blown about by unseen forces in your shadow. As long as the contents of your shadow remain unconscious and unexamined, you can struggle with addictions, self-sabotaging behaviors, and dysfunctional relationship patterns. You will unconsciously act from childhood wounds. Your perceptions, thoughts, beliefs, and emotions will be unconsciously distorted by demons hidden in your shadow.

Psychedelics function like a microscope, magnifying demons that hide in your shadow. Those who imagine that all psychedelic journeys would be trippy, cosmic experiences of light, love, and magical transformation will often abandon psychedelics once they encounter their shadow. Only those who are highly motivated will welcome the opportunity to face their demons.

"You cannot get to the promised land if you are not willing to go through the wilderness." ~ T.D. Jakes

Breaking Through Denial and Dissociation

Denial and dissociation are coping mechanisms that banish memories of intolerable traumatic events to shadow realms. Denial is a psychological defense that rejects and represses conscious awareness of a traumatic event or events. We may deny that an event occurred or we may minimize its impact because the emotions that come with truly acknowledging it are too painful or scary to feel. Psychedelics break the spell of denial, allowing denied feelings and memories to surface.

Dissociation is a psychological defense that disconnects you from the unbearable horror of trauma. It allows you to "be absent" during traumatic experiences. It is a survival mechanism that blocks the experience from entering conscious awareness and prevents annihilation of the psyche. The experience of trauma is frozen and stored in the unconscious psyche and the body to shield you from having to suffer the full impact of the trauma as a whole. Psychedelics can melt walls of amnesia to expose memories, sensations, and feelings that were split off from conscious awareness.

When an overwhelming event happens that we are not sufficiently resourced to deal with, we slam shut an internal door to protect us from its demons. When psychedelics open the door, all the demons are still there, just as scary and overwhelming as when we shut the door on them.

Even with the help of MDMA to soften defenses and anxiety, most people are initially afraid to open the door. They fear that if they open their own personal Pandora's box, they will be flooded with pain or anger they will be unable to handle.

Those who were childhood victims of adult rage may be afraid of their anger. They could have learned that expressing anger at perpetrators is dangerous; such expression could have jeopardized their connection to adults they depended on for survival. They may fear if they access their anger, they will act out their rage in uncontrollable ways that will hurt or alienate people.

Those who are afraid of their emotional pain may fear that if they open to their pain in any way, they will become seriously depressed and unable to function. They may need assurance that the psyche will open the door just a little at a time, as they are ready. They may also need reminding that the pain they are uncovering is probably old, childhood pain they were too fragile to feel when they were young. Emotions that overwhelm children are manageable for adults. It is safe to feel and express feelings in a supportive, therapeutic environment. Those who are willing to feel their deepest pain are rewarded with the greatest life-changing transformation.

"What the caterpillar calls the end of the world, the Master calls a butterfly" ~ Richard Bach

The amazing ability of psychedelics to penetrate psychological defenses and bring shadow material to consciousness is precisely why recreational use can sometimes lead to a treacherous "bad trip." A novice expecting to have a fun, party experience will be unprepared and frightened if scary shadow material emerges. If they manage to abort the process, they may have recurring, disturbing flashbacks long after the drug wears off.

Most initial journeys are eye-opening, peak experiences. Allow trust, safety, and resources to build with gentle, healing journeys before introducing stronger meds with intention focused on working through shadow material.

Accessing Traumatic Memory

As you navigate beyond your defenses, psychedelics will shine a spotlight into the dark corners of your psyche, bringing to consciousness relevant material that is ready to process. Memories you have forgotten, denied, never felt or assimilated may begin to surface.

Memories can arise spontaneously or be triggered by current events in your life. Talking about your issues or looking at photos from childhood can also bring up memories. For example, a journeyer talks about his fears in a new relationship. The sitter inquires about the fear's origin. Suddenly, the journeyer recalls a long-forgotten, teenage, first love that ended in heartbreak. "I had no idea that affected me so much!" he exclaims. Immersed in memory, he feels the full, painful impact of the rejection and loss for the first time. "Now I can see I've kept my heart closed. I never wanted to risk being hurt like that again."

Traumatic memories often manifest as emotions or bodily sensations and behaviors--sometimes without words or story. As memories surface, you may cry, sob, wail, or scream. You might become chilled, tremble, spasm, or thrash about. Your teeth may chatter, your legs may run in place. You may suddenly become weak and unable to move. You may experience nausea, retching, coughing, flu-like symptoms, and rapid breathing. This deep feeling and releasing can go on for hours. The cathartic expression of emotions and somatic tensions while reliving repressed traumatic events is called "abreaction." Even if no narrative or visual memories are recalled, abreaction is a form of memory release.

As you stay with primal feelings and sensations, relevant cognitive memory may surface. Denied events may be vividly recalled. A myriad of fresh memories may pop up that you have never recalled or thought about before. You may find yourself spontaneously age regressed, experiencing emotions you felt as a vulnerable little child. You may be transported back in time to experience feelings, sensations and body memories of traumatic events passed on to you from ancestors or past lives.

For some, memories and associated expressions unfold in age-related, chronological order. Each journey picks up where the last one left off. For instance, in one journey you may navigate through infant issues; in the following journey you may deal with toddler issues.

Memories may also unfold in reverse chronological order, with more current incidents arising first.

Memories of dissociated events will usually be more fragmented and less explicit than denied events. Dissociated events are generally not recalled as a narrative with a beginning, middle, and end. They are more likely to emerge as intense emotions, physical sensations, sensory impressions, symbolic enactments, or fleeting images. You may have a felt sense of knowing what is being experienced. A felt sense is an intuitive, bodily knowledge that is not yet formed into thought or words. Because dissociated traumatic memories were never consciously experienced or recorded in a linear way in the cerebral cortex, they may initially be hard to believe. Learn to let material surface without stopping to understand or question its validity.

Trauma from early, pre-verbal childhood can be accessed, felt, and released, but may never have concrete memories attached. The experience may not be translatable into communicable language. This is because infants' brains and nervous systems have not developed the capacity to record memory in explicit words and images. Trauma from infancy may sometimes be replicated in transference within the therapeutic relationship. Pre-verbal trauma may also emerge as archetypal images and stories that represent events or interpersonal dynamics between infant and parents or caretakers.

If needed, the sitter may help the journeyer make sense of, and process through, their experience by asking questions like: "If what you are feeling had words and could speak, I wonder what it might say." If fragments of memories emerge, the sitter may probe to expand the memories by asking questions like: "Then what happens?" "How old do you feel?" "Who else is there with you?" "Is it night or day?" and so on. Such questioning helps flesh out the traumatic event into a coherent story that the journeyer can integrate into conscious awareness.

Since traumatic memories may only be accessible with the help of psychedelics, the rational mind may doubt or dismiss their validity. Thoughts like "I'm making this up," "It's not real," or "It's just the drug" are common until further compelling evidence becomes convincing. It may be helpful for the sitter to explain that psychedelics are tools that magnify hidden, unconscious material like microscopes magnify micro-worlds hidden from the naked eye.

A sitter should assume that all memories are based on truth, even if the journeyer doubts them. It is important that these discoveries be acknowledged and validated. New memories of trauma can be shocking and must be allowed to come up at an organic pace that allows them to be gradually accepted and digested. A sitter must NEVER lead this process by prematurely filling in the blanks or creating a story before journeyers are ready to discover the truth for themselves.

For example, a psychologically savvy sitter may detect convincing clues of childhood sexual abuse as the journeyer talks about sexual issues, fears, fantasies, and phobias. When repressed abuse material begins to surface, the journeyer may start having glimpses and vague memories of events. This process often begins with memories of feeling uncomfortable, scared, or "icky" around certain people. The journeyer's body may involuntarily assume positions that appear to be body memories that replicate sexual abuse. If the journeyer is unable to make sense of these feelings and involuntary behaviors in journey after journey, the sitter can help them connect the dots of emerging phenomena by reporting observable clues and introducing the possibility of sexual abuse. "Many people who have experienced what you are experiencing now were sexually abused as children," might be appropriate to say, but only if the journeyer is ready and resourced enough to deal with this information. The sitter should NEVER authoritatively declare anything like, "You were sexually abused by your father," before the journeyer has recovered convincing memories for him or herself.

As new, traumatic, childhood memories surface, previously held beliefs of having had a reasonably happy, normal childhood fade. This may shatter tenaciously held fantasies about parents and caretakers. Every child is born with a hard-wired survival instinct to bond with parents or caregivers. It is a psychological imperative for children to believe that they are wanted, loved, protected, and cared for. When this is not their experience, they must deny their true feelings and create a fantasy of idealized parents. This fantasy bond defense can be extremely hard to crack in mainstream talk therapy. The ability of psychedelics to pierce through denial allows the truth to emerge. When the truth is exposed, the healing process can begin.

Lisa was seriously overweight and depressed. She struggled with an eating disorder. During her second MDMA journey, she focused into her body and gave this report.

"My whole body is tingling and quivering. I feel tightness in my chest. It feels like there's an iron shield protecting my heart from being hurt. My heart is sad. There's a knot in my stomach--as I breathe into it I feel lonely. Ow! It hurts! Every time my Dad hurt me it felt like a knife stab in my stomach. I didn't want to feel it--I want to eat to stop the pain. My whole pelvis feels numb. I don't like feeling inside my body--there's so much pain here. I see how disconnected I've been from it." Lisa spent hours sobbing and releasing the terror, pain, shame, and rage of early childhood incest. During another session, she experienced memories of leaving her body when the abuse became overwhelming: "I feel strange, light headed. I feel dizzy, out of control. Feels like I'm spinning all around the room. Once I give up fighting, I feel peaceful--numb all over. It feels kind of pleasant. I'm detached from feelings of what he's doing to me. Where's my body? I feel my spirit leave. My body is just a piece of meat at this point. If I stay disconnected he can't hurt me."

Navigating Through Trauma

Choosing the Right Meds

Everyone responds differently to every medicine and every medicine has its own unique properties. A strongly defended journeyer will initially need higher dosages to get results. For those with a sensitive constitution, higher doses may be overwhelming. The ideal protocol softens psychological defenses and habitual needs to be in control. An effective dose should fully immerse the person into the journey experience, and be strong enough to access unconscious material and promote releasing of trauma.

MDMA is essential for lowering defenses and assuring a safe passage through trauma. If MDMA alone does not achieve the desired destination, consider gradually introducing stronger meds.

LSD will cut through denial and amplify deeper layers of unconscious material. WARNING! LSD can transport a person into their deepest, darkest, most traumatic memories. Those who have significant childhood trauma may find LSD to be stark and brutal in higher doses. For this reason, sitters should start beginners with a conservative 50 mcg to 100 mcg dose.

Taking 50 to 100 mg of MDMA at the beginning of an LSD session will allow journeyers to stay present with unfolding traumatic memories without spacing out or getting overwhelmed. Take MDMA first, then wait thirty to sixty minutes before adding LSD. This allows the MDMA to soften defenses before the LSD takes effect. An additional dose of 50 to 100 mg of MDMA may be added an hour or so into the session. The effects of LSD last longer than MDMA; therefore, additional MDMA may be needed to soften defenses for the duration of the journey. If the introductory-dose LSD session is tolerated well, it can be increased gradually in each future journey until an optimum working dose is reached.

Psilocybin can access and release trauma in a warmer, more organic way than LSD, and with less danger of re-traumatization if doses are kept moderate. The healing intelligence of mushrooms works in paradigms beyond the scope of psychotherapeutic models. Those who are new to psilocybin should start with a cautious dose of two or three grams. To lower defenses and insure the deepest possible experience, beginners can take 50 to 100 mg of MDMA first, then take psilocybin about an hour later. Once a journeyer is comfortable with the mushroom experience, it may be safe to try psilocybin by itself in subsequent journeys.

For those who are more experienced, LSD combined with psilocybin can be an effective protocol for releasing trauma. Beginning the session with LSD greatly amplifies unconscious material. It allows the journeyer to sharply focus into places in the body where trauma is stored. Adding a moderate dose of psilocybin about an hour after taking LSD promotes further discharge and healing of trauma.

The type and dose of medicines that work best for a journeyer will most likely change as they proceed along the healing path. If they get stuck in an impasse where results are dwindling, experiment with different meds.

Here is an example of how one might choose the right meds:

Let's say that you, the journeyer, have ample prior experience working with MDMA, LSD, and Psilocybin in your therapy. You and your sitter/therapist are familiar with how each medicine affects you and what dosages work best for you.

As your healing process unfolds, you become aware that there is a troublesome issue or place in your body that needs further exploration and healing. You feel lots of fear and resistance to embarking on such a journey, so you decide you will start the session with 90 mg of MDMA. This dose is just enough to insure a safe passage through your initial defenses without candy coating shadow material that may need to be felt and processed.

Next, you plan to take a 100 mcg dose of LSD thirty to forty-five minutes later, allowing time for the MDMA to start lowering defenses before the LSD takes effect. From experience, you know this dose of LSD is high enough to bring unconscious material to conscious awareness, yet moderate enough for you to be able to stay focused and embodied.

Finally, you decide you'll add three grams of psilocybin an hour after taking the LSD, allowing time for the LSD to amplify unconscious material before the mushrooms take effect. From experience, you know that this light dose of psilocybin is just enough to enhance the release of trauma and add an extra dimension of healing that mushrooms often provide. A higher dose of mushrooms might take the journey into disembodied realms that could distract you from your intended focus. Through this trial and error process, you and your therapist/sitter find a protocol that best moves you toward your therapeutic goals.

Focusing in Your Body

"The body's life is the life of sensations and emotions. The body feels real hunger, real thirst, real joy in the sun or the snow, real pleasure in the smell of roses or the look of a lilac bush, real anger, real sorrow, real tenderness, real warmth, real passion, real hate, real grief. All the emotions belong in the body and are only recognized by the mind." ~ D.H. Lawrence

Unhealed trauma gets frozen and stored in various parts of the body. Therefore, to heal trauma you must focus your attention back into your body. If you habitually live in your head, focusing inside your body during a journey will require diligent discipline.

Dissociation from the body is not just a phenomenon reserved for survivors of trauma. Living in your head has become the norm. The internet and omnipresent media keep us constantly engaged in our heads. Exaltation of the intellect has produced a culture of adults who live largely in worlds of thoughts and images. Being present in one's body is a subjective experience that cannot be scientifically quantified. As a result, most people commonly assume they are more in their bodies than they actually are. Most of us relate to our body as a machine-like extension of our brain. We push it to perform according to our will, with little awareness of its inner depth and mystery.

To explore your inner body during journeys, close your eyes and focus your attention on body sensations. Be aware of the gentle rising and falling of your chest and belly with each breath. Feel your heart beat. Be aware of the mass your body occupies in space. Feel the weight of your body being supported by what you're sitting or lying on. Notice if the right and left sides of your body feel different. Feel sensations as you touch various parts of your body. Feel pleasurable sensations on your skin from subtle breezes, contact with fabrics, and so on.

As psychedelics amplify body sensations, you may become aware of chronic muscle tension and unconscious armoring. Let your body stretch, move, dance, tremble, spasm, or roll about to release this tension. Trust your body's intuition. Don't think about it.

Scan your attention inside your body from head to toes. See if you can find places that feel relaxed, tingly, alive, and pleasurable. Spend time letting good sensations in. Then look for places that feel painful, numb, jittery, tight, or heavy. These unpleasant sensations are your body's way of saying "Pay attention here." When you find these places, focus your attention there. What sensations or emotions do you feel there? Imagine that with each inhale you are breathing new life and healing into these problem areas.

As your breath softens chronic muscular armor, the trauma underneath can be felt and discharged. Allow all emotions, visions, memories, insights, and involuntary movements to surface. Symptoms from old injuries or surgeries sometimes materialize to be felt and released. Trust the wisdom of your body and psyche to process and clear trauma.

There may be pockets of trauma stored in various places in your body. You may discover trauma hidden in dissociated parts of your body that were split off from conscious awareness. The belly and heart center in the middle of your chest are common places where old emotional pain and fear may be stored. You might get visuals of some sort of wall or protective covering over your heart that has been keeping it closed. Imagine using your breath to open it. Be willing to feel any heartbreak, betrayal, and grief that caused your heart to wall up.

You may need the concentration of a Zen master to stay focused on places in your body that contain highly defended, traumatic memories. You will need to narrow your awareness like a laser beam, shining the light of your attention into targeted areas. You may strongly resist feeling distressing, scary emotions and sensations that arise from these places. If your attention wanders, you may need coaching from your sitter to stay focused. Nurturing physical contact, massage, or bodywork from your sitter may help keep the healing process moving.

During a combination MDMA/LSD journey, a woman had this experience while focusing in her body:

"My heart is aching. It feels numb. It feels like I want to cry but I can't. Now I am feeling a hole in my stomach. It's like a bullet hole where I've been shot. It's awful! I don't want to feel this pain. I want to scream." She screams and kicks her legs as she is immersed in memories of being raped by her father. "Now my heart feels heavy. Where were you, Mom? You did nothing to stop it. Not once. Never! I knew Dad didn't love me but I still wanted your love. I'm feeling so sad. I was in denial. I thought I loved my Mom, but I really don't. Now I'm realizing how numb I've been, how I shut my feelings down, how guarded my heart has been. There is a longing for something that wasn't. I'm feeling melancholy. The hole in my stomach was all the love and affection I never got from my parents. I'm working on letting my heart open now."

Discharging Fear

Unconscious fear from unhealed trauma can severely impair your health and well-being. Symptoms include generalized anxiety, muscle tension, sleep disturbances, digestive problems, difficulty concentrating, and avoidance of situations that resemble past traumatic events.

When you are on the verge of accessing unhealed trauma, you may experience a flood of intense anxiety. This means you are getting close to scary, painful feelings that once threatened your very survival as a child. You may want to flee, engage in distractions, or end the journey. MDMA lowers anxiety and helps you pass through this defensive layer of fear.

Once you navigate beyond the initial rush of anxiety, your body may start releasing fear from past traumatic events. You may feel waves of terror coursing through your body. Your breathing may accelerate. Your teeth might chatter. Your body may tremble or convulse. You may become nauseous or chilled. You might experience speedy, electric current sensations of adrenalin running through your body--sometimes accompanied by intense vibrations with high or low pitched tones. You are releasing fear by feeling these sensations, even if there is no story or emotion attached.

The discharging of fear may ebb and flow for hours during journeys. There may be layers of fear and it may require multiple journeys to release them. This is a healing process. It's the body's way of letting go of accumulated fear. Let it happen.

A patient sought treatment for recurring panic attacks. For six months she had lived in constant dread, never knowing when another episode would strike. In public or when falling asleep at night, her heart would suddenly start pounding. She'd gasp for air, terrified she was having a fatal heart attack. Her doctor prescribed Xanex, but she did not want to continue being dependent on the drug. We had already established a trusting therapeutic relationship during our prior journeywork together, so we decided to try an MDMA session. About an hour into her journey, she became very frightened and cold. I covered her with blankets and held her hand. Then her body started violently shaking and thrashing about. MDMA and the safety of my comforting presence allowed her to move through her terror of dying from a heart attack. There were waves of fear and trembling throughout the session as we processed through underlying sources of stress that were at the root of her anxiety attacks. A month later she reported that she'd had no more anxiety attacks since the journey.

Discharging Anger

Children who are abused by adults or bullied by peers are often too powerless or scared to protest or retaliate with righteous anger. Children who are neglected, shamed, or abandoned generally have little idea they deserve better. In both cases, the primal fight response to trauma is repressed.

When the sitter can sense a journeyer's repressed anger escalating, its expression should be encouraged--the more primal and cathartic, the better. The sitter can suggest giving voice to the anger by roaring or growling like a big, powerful animal, or yelling words like "No!" "Stop!" and " I hate you!" The sitter can encourage the journeyer to vent in some visceral way, like screaming, kicking, or hitting. At first, journeyers may feel silly or uncomfortable doing this. If attempts at hitting a punching bag or pillow are lackluster, or result in collapsing into tears and powerlessness, the sitter may suggest "fake it 'til you make it" or using Method acting tactics. When the journeyer thinks about something that makes them angry, then primes the pump by going through the motions of hitting or screaming, they can cause authentic rage to kick in.

If the journeyer can't get beyond a personal taboo against expressing anger directly at a perpetrator, the sitter may get things rolling by invoking the journeyer's anger at some person, institution, or organization they are angry at right now. Global issues like political corruption, treatment of minorities, animal cruelty, etc. may help trigger anger.

Sometimes, anger is blocked by fear. Journeyers may be afraid that if they open the floodgates of rage, they will kill people or become just like their scary, angry perpetrators. The sitter may need to reassure the journeyer that venting anger in a therapeutic setting is safe and important for healing.

Spiritual people may have been taught to deny anger by concealing it under a sugary frosting of premature forgiveness. They may need assurance that venting righteous anger in therapy hurts no one and will eventually lead to genuine forgiveness.

If attempts to induce the expression of anger fail, don't force it. If it needs to be felt and vented, it will erupt at another time in the journeyer's healing process. For some, anger may not be accessible until they have come out of denial about their childhood pain. Once they have felt the full impact of the abuse or neglect, they will have something to be angry about.

Once repressed anger has been unleashed in journeyspace, a person may become hyper-sensitive in anger- provoking situations for days or weeks after a journey. The slightest irritation may cause an explosion of anger. When the floodgates of a lifetime of suppressed anger open, there may be a tidal wave of pent up rage that needs to be honored, felt, and expressed before it dissipates.

If this happens to you, don't panic. This stage will pass. Make sure you have a safe way of venting, like hitting and screaming into pillows. A self-defense class may be an effective venue to discharge anger and feel empowered. You might want to warn people around you not to take your outbursts personally. Let them know this is a temporary part of your healing process.

Timid individuals who habitually suppress, deny, or sublimate their anger, often experience their rage as an empowering, exhilarating feeling that builds healthy assertiveness and self-worth. At a primal level, anger affirms that "I matter. Treat me with respect and kindness."

A woman in her forties had a pattern of getting into relationships with abusive men. She never felt anger when boyfriends abused or betrayed her. During her journey on LSD and MDMA she notices the mean streak her dad and ex-boyfriend have in common. She starts feeling nauseous. Her body trembles in fear as new memories of her father emerge:

"Dad is shoving me down the hall. He is over me--pinching me. I am pinned against the wall. No escape. He's unreasonable. You never knew when he'd get triggered. I'd seen him hit my Mom. I lived in constant fear."

I (the sitter) encourage her to get angry at her Dad. She screams and beats a punching bag. The intensity of her venting builds to a primal rage. It's the first time she has ever expressed anger. Months after her journey, she sent me this email:

"I've found my anger! I mean really found it! I was in a pissy mood for a long time after the journey where I felt anger for the first time. I was pissed off and had no idea why until I remembered you warning me I might be easily irritated after opening the door to my anger. As soon as I realized what was going on, the pissy mood went away. In its place I felt a sense of enormous strength! I was filled with a don't-mess-with-me feeling. It is absolutely incredible! I love it!"

Empowered by accessing her anger, this woman was able to break old, ineffectual patterns. She is now in a healthy relationship with a wonderful man. Nobody messes with her anymore.

Embracing Emotional Pain

"All our neuroses are substitutes for legitimate suffering." ~ Carl Jung

Healthy children openly express a full range of emotions. They scream and throw tantrums when they are angry. They cry when they hurt. They giggle and squeal with joy when they are happy. Their hearts are full of love and bubbling with enthusiasm for the adventure of life.

If you were a child who was abused, neglected, abandoned, or betrayed, you most likely shut the door to your heart to block out the pain. You may have learned to ignore your pain if your suffering was ignored by your caretakers. You might have been told shaming axioms like "Boys don't cry" "You're too sensitive" or "Stop being a baby." You may have spent years medicating your sadness in order to function and put on a happy social face. You might experience chronic depression but be unable to heal the origin of your sadness. You might avoid deep emotional intimacy to prevent being hurt again.

When psychedelics open your heart all the pain is still there, just as fresh and intense as the day you shut the door on it.

As your heart opens, you may uncover painful, new memories. You may encounter layers of old grief, hopelessness, and despair. You may feel the pain of not feeling seen, loved, and protected by parents. You might feel losses of loved ones and pets you never grieved. You may mourn the loss of childhood innocence and the lost years you've spent floundering. As you awaken from denial, you may feel the pain and suffering of all living beings.

Pain you medicated with addictions or antidepressants must now be felt and released in order to heal. It's not crucial to associate the pain with any particular memory or story. There may be a huge reservoir of undifferentiated or preverbal pain that needs to be felt. During your journey, crying, wailing, and sobbing can sometimes go on for hours. Crying and sobbing are ways the body releases sadness and heals old wounds. Let it happen. For some, this grieving can feel like an exquisite purge that opens their heart and validates their humanity.

Once wounds are laid bare in journeyspace, you may feel sad for days or weeks following your journey. Surrender to the grieving process. Give yourself down time to cry. Listen to sad music or watch sad movies that promote tears. Resist old patterns of keeping busy in order to avoid, stuff, or ignore painful feelings.

If you have a history of depression, you might be reluctant to feel your pain. You may fear you'll never come back from the sadness. Know that once all your old sadness is truly felt, you will be free of it forever.

As you uncover layers of pain, you may become temporarily age-regressed and less functional as an adult. You may need time to comfort, pamper and communicate with your hurting, inner-child self.

Some journeyers have suicidal thoughts and feelings arise during their healing process. If this happens to you, it's probably a sign that you are getting close to core wounds. It usually means repressed pain from your past is coming up to be felt and healed. Suicidal moods will pass if you allow yourself to feel them. If suicidal feelings become overwhelming, contact your therapist or a suicide hotline.

Addictions may temporarily resurface as the psyche attempts to medicate or manage the emerging pain. If this happens, be compassionate. Don't beat yourself up. Temporarily reverting to familiar, self-soothing addictions may be necessary as a resource to help you move through overwhelmingly painful parts of your healing process. If you are acting out excessively, seek out extra therapy and support to help you through these tough times.

The soul of a child thrives in the environment of parental love. To escape the unbearable pain of not being truly loved and wanted, psychological defenses sequester the soul within protective walls, creating an existential void at one's core. As layers of defenses are stripped away in journeywork, you may encounter this as a terrifying abyss. To rescue your soul, you must be willing to plunge into the void to feel and release the pain.

Wounds take time to heal. Be patient and compassionate with yourself. Don't expect yourself to feel and process through all your pain in a journey or two. Your psyche can handle only a little at a time. Don't force your hurting inner child to feel more pain than he or she is ready to feel.

Shadow work is like psychological detoxing. As toxic trauma is being cleared, you will most likely feel worse before you feel better.

You are being remodeled. Your old structure is being torn down in order for a healthy new structure to be built. It's going to be messy and take a while. At the end of the process, your willingness to feel your deepest pain opens your heart to love and joy again.

A fifty-year-old father was told by his therapist and wife that he was emotionally disconnected. Here are excerpts from one of his early LSD sessions:

"Emotional detachment, what does it mean? Was it Mom? How could she go through her whole life and never say 'I love you' to me or my sister? All she had to say was 'You're doing OK, you're my boy, I'm proud of you.' She never hugged or complimented me. I was never good enough. She made me feel worthless.

"How does it feel when your mother doesn't love you? Am I disconnected? I need to feel this. Oh my God, I feel the pain right in my chest! I'm falling into the abyss. I feel it in my whole body. I understand; this is pain. This is sorrow and deep, deep loss. I feel tears all around me. Buckets of tears. I had no idea I had this pain and sorrow. This is not crying, it's like weeping--so much deeper. I've been carrying this bag for too long. Let it go!

"Now I am being filled up. This must be my heart. My heart is opening! This has to be what it feels like to love! How absolutely beautiful! I have never felt this before. What a terrible waste of time. Why did I go through life that way? How can we walk through life half asleep? My God, I had no idea--none. No shit, emotionally disconnected! How can I ever be the same? Breathe; breathe deep. I am having consistent feelings of purging my pain and being filled with love. It is so wonderful! There are no words that can describe what I'm going through now. I'm walking in the garden of Eden with my wife and kids. It's paradise! So beautiful! I felt pain that I never admitted was there. Never have I felt such sorrow and pain--but also happiness. I feel like I'm born again. I have another chance."

Moving Through Shadow

As you move through your shadow, memories of trauma will pop up like ghosts from your past. Each ghost will evoke layers of emotion. At first you will feel afraid. You may have run from these scary feelings most of your life. Next, you might feel a layer of anger erupt. Finally, you uncover a layer of emotional pain hidden under the anger. Sometimes you may feel the pain before you get to the anger. Once the pain is felt and cleared, another ghost from your past may materialize, triggering new memories and more layers of emotion.

You might discover different types of trauma from different ages. Initial journeys may bring up early childhood abandonment wounds. Subsequent journeys may reveal abuse wounds from adolescence.

As new layers of unhealed material surface, you may encounter new layers of defenses. To surmount these defenses you may need to increase dosages or change which meds you use. Including MDMA in your protocol always helps soften stubborn defenses.

At some points in your journeys, you may feel like you are going crazy. This most commonly happens on higher doses of psilocybin or LSD. Don't panic. This could be part of the transformational process called "ego death" that is explained later in this guide. The feeling of going crazy may also be part of remembering and releasing the confusion and unbearable pain that originally overwhelmed your mind. If you are experiencing craziness, focus your attention outside of the turmoil in your head. Stay centered in your body and your breath. As you feel and release the trauma, the craziness will eventually pass. This is a healing process. Let it happen.

Your psychological and social development may have been impaired by childhood trauma. As you heal, you may need to learn skills from missed developmental stages. For example, if your wounds prevented you from healthy adolescent dating, you might now need to navigate this arena like a beginner.

If you are dealing with sexual abuse issues, your sexual libido may flat-line for periods of time during your healing process. This can be especially worrisome for men. Don't be alarmed. As you continue healing, your interest in sex will be renewed. You may become aware of old patterns of unhealthy sexual behavior that were unconscious reenactments of your sexual abuse. You may need a period of abstinence to rewire addictive and/or impersonal sexual habits.

If you are feeling and releasing trauma in your journeywork, your body and psyche may want to continue the healing process for days or weeks after your session. Give yourself time and space to honor emerging emotions, sensations, and somatic discharging.

If you have been deeply wounded, your journey through shadow might be a slow process that takes years. Deep healing is an organic, feminine process analogous to birthing a baby. It takes nine months to create a baby. You can't rush the job because you want it faster.

The trajectory of the healing path is seldom a straight line. You might take three steps forward, then seem to fall one step back when unexpected road blocks or new layers of unhealed material appear. You may get frustrated and worried if your therapeutic goals are not realized quickly. Be patient. Results from inner work may not show up in your life for a while. The healing process is similar to a caterpillar's metamorphosis. You can't see a pupa transforming inside its cocoon until it emerges as a butterfly. Similarly, you may not be able to spread your new wings and fly until your inner healing process is complete.

For survivors of major traumas, it may seem like the wounds are too great and the trauma releasing will go on forever. It's easy to lose hope. It may be helpful to consider that you're probably the first person in your family to heal from generations of dysfunction. According to the new science of epigenetics, you likely inherited trauma from the DNA of your ancestors. Healing multi-generational wounds is like stopping a train that has been building speed for decades. And, who knows? You may have been dealing with these issues and wounds for many lifetimes. Expect it to take a while.

As layers of trauma are peeled away, you may get glimpses of your core essence underneath. If you were not valued or treated with love and respect as a child you may feel--deep down inside--that you are inferior, unlovable, or bad. As these false identities drop away, your pure spirit is free to blossom. Enjoy taking time to discover and explore your emerging new Self.

12. RESOURCING

You need nutritious food and a good night's sleep to rejuvenate for another active day. Similarly, you need recharging, support, and restorative breaks to get through arduous shadow work. This is called "resourcing."

A toddler learns to separate from mommy by going a few feet away from her, then running back to the comfort and safety of her arms. The ability to run back allows the toddler to go a few feet farther the next time. So it is with trauma healing work. To safely process through trauma, you need to be able to pendulate back and forth between focusing on trauma, allowing resourcing, then returning to the trauma. Taking time to stop, rest, play, joke, and find safety will allow the next layer of trauma work to take place.

The following are examples of resources you can draw upon to help you through tortuous journeys.

1. Pleasurable sensory stimuli: Take breaks to appreciate beautiful music, art, flowers, and other sensory delights. If you are journeying where you have easy access to a private back yard or garden, spend some time outdoors. Because psychedelics can amplify sensual pleasure, you might experience ordinary stimuli to be exquisite. A back yard may become an enchanting wonderland.

2. Memories of times and places where you felt happy and safe: Immerse yourself in memories of idyllic settings in nature or holidays at Grandma's house, for instance. You may also use your imagination to create a personal "safe space" that can include magical landscapes, people, animals, deities, etc.

3. Current and/or previous sources of love and comfort: Bring to mind favorite relatives, caretakers, friends, spouses, or pets. Sometimes, good memories may be buried in your past and long forgotten. Search for them. If you were raised by parents or caretakers who were neglectful or abusive, there still might be some bright moments worth remembering and feeling.

4. Connection to a comforting, protective Higher Power: Much has already been documented about how psychedelics can promote a profound connection to your Higher Self, God, spirit guides, and the like. You may or may not have such an experience. If you do, it will likely resonate with your own prior beliefs and exposure to spirituality. Faith in a Higher Power will support you through any challenge.

Men tend to believe that cathartic trauma releasing alone will heal them. In time, this foolhardy, macho approach often backfires. It's like driving your car to a distant destination without stopping to fill the gas tank.

Take time to relax and recharge between journeys. Seek out resources like support groups, therapy, bodywork, supportive friends, and sources of spiritual inspiration. Get some fun exercise.

Eat good, healthy food. Get a massage. Hang out with pets. Spend time in nature. Make space in your busy schedule to do things you enjoy. Allow at least two weeks between journeys.

Some people survive trauma by becoming emotionally numb. They are unable to experience pleasure or joy in ordinary activities. For these people, feel-good MDMA journeys may be an essential resource.

An MDMA journey can be a healing, restorative, mini-vacation. Your intent for such a journey might be to let go of stress, relax chronic tension, and focus on pleasure. If possible, get comforted by a caring loved one. Let in tender, soothing touch you may never have received as a child. This feminine aspect of healing is every bit as powerful and productive as cathartic, masculine, shadow work.

The following personal experience is an example of a resourcing journey.

"In the summer of 1988, a dear old boyfriend and I took a boat trip to Catalina Island with the intention of having an MDMA resourcing day. I was weary from working through childhood trauma in my journeywork. We were both facing stressful, troubling times in our lives.

"We hired a taxi to take us far from town to a secluded bluff overlooking the ocean. It was a perfect, warm, sunny day. We found a beautiful spot, got comfortable, and took MDMA. We talked some, but mostly sat silently, gazing at the sunlight shimmering on the vast ocean stretched out before us. Our minds were still, our bodies were relaxed. Hours passed. We were immersed in a blissful, timeless paradise. The sublime experience of tranquility, contentment, and communion with nature rejuvenated our spirits.

"As late afternoon began to get chilly, I asked my friend to hold me as we beheld the glorious sunset. As I sank into his arms, my chronic, defensive armoring melted. I had a profound experience of letting love into my unloved, inner child for the first time in my life."

13. BEYOND THE EGO

"You don't have a soul, you are a soul. You have a body." ~ C.S. Lewis

Experiencing "Ego Death"

At some point in your journeys you may suddenly feel like you are dying or going crazy. This most commonly happens on higher doses of psilocybin or LSD, as mentioned earlier in this guide. This harrowing experience may be part of a transformational process called "ego death." It's not actual death, nor a death of the healthy ego. It's an experience of letting go of rigid identification with your body, mind, biographical story, and the concepts you have used to define yourself.

When the ego death process begins, you'll most likely experience great fear and confusion. As you move beyond your familiar sense of self, you may encounter a frightful inner void. Don't panic. If you let go into the void, you will eventually experience your true, essential Self, beyond the confines of body, mind, ego, space, and time.

Ego death can be an immediate experience or a process that unfolds over time. Those who traverse this territory generally come away with an expansive, new perspective on life. They become less fear-driven. Their fears of death fade. Realms of mystical and spiritual experience become more tangible. They are able to live more peacefully and joyfully in the moment.

"If you have identified with your soul while you're alive, death is just another moment." ~ Ram Dass

A thirty-nine year old woman gave this account of her transcendent experience on LSD and psilocybin.

"I saw a golden light, I went beyond ego, Higher Self, confusion--beyond what I can describe in words, beyond God and me, beyond duality--infinite. It's like a paradigm shift. How do I make sense of all this? Be simple. Go back to childlike innocence and love."

A young woman was able to attribute most of her fear, sadness, and depression to her fear of death. Her dreams indicated it was time to deal with this issue. She wondered what might be gained by encountering death and returning. She approached her fourth journey with an intention to have a death experience. The following is her report of her experience on 5.5 grams of psilocybin.

"I was descending, ever so slowly, into an abyss. My mother, father, and our family home were the only threads I held onto during this period of my session. I tried to summon the will to steer the journey toward my boyfriend, possibly in an attempt to move the journey to more comfortable and comprehensible ground. His face appeared hazy and left quickly. I tried to remember anything I could about him, which at this point seemed nearly impossible. I felt myself detaching from everything familiar in my life, a process that was leaving me feeling extremely ungrounded.

"Some time passed while I traveled the universe. My focus turned toward trying to bring myself back to my life. However, the more I tried, the more confused and frightened I became at the understanding that it was slipping farther and farther away. My parents' names and personalities were gone from memory. I could not recall my boyfriend's identity. Finally, I could not remember my own name or virtually anything about who I was as a human being. I was sinking very quickly and fell into a state of panic. I said, 'I think I'm going crazy.'

"I was alone and in the dark. I had completely detached from my body. The only way I knew I existed, that I was something, somewhere, was because I could hear myself breathing. My terror began to fade slightly and as I sat in this place, I began to accept that I was completely alone in oblivion, and I could possibly remain here forever. A beautiful sensation of acceptance of this fact overcame me. Mild relief replaced some of my panic as I listened to the sound of aloneness, my own breath. I remember thinking, 'I could die here and never return.' Then aloud, I whispered, 'It's OK if I die. It's OK if I die.' This moment of complete acceptance of death was the pinnacle of my journey.

"The journey acted as a paradigm blaster that allowed me to view my current life template through a different theoretical lens.

The medicine pulled me down past my daily concerns and struggles and brought me to the ultimate moment of fear: my death. Once experienced and accepted, the medicine began my ascent back into ego consciousness. The medicine taught me that I can enter and accept perceived permanent aloneness and nothingness, and with that knowledge, I can return to the world in which I currently exist--and live in it differently. The high stakes of this world having fallen, life decisions and events feel less dire. The medicine also taught me to disengage from attachments and the need for certainty in this realm. In essence, entering and returning from oblivion substantially reduced my anxiety because of the new lens through which I view my existence. When I am anxious now, it is a signal that the unknown is calling. I can then practice a transit to that place, disengage myself from my current reality, and be reminded that I will be all right when my physical death finally comes, and realize that the realm in which I walk now is one of an infinite number. This knowledge grounds me in a deeper place of being."

14. AFTER THE JOURNEY

If you have taken MDMA during your journey, you may feel depleted afterward. MDMA is generally harder on the body than LSD, psilocybin, or marijuana. There are many anecdotal suggestions about how to best repair the body after an MDMA journey. Do your own research. Find what works best for you. More information can be found at www.erowid.org.

Always eat a little healthy food after journeys, even if you don't feel like eating. Choose something easy to eat and digest, like fruit, yogurt, or soup. Include something with protein to refuel and ground after strenuous, draining journeywork.

The end of the journey can often be a time of deep reflection. Spend quiet time with yourself. Be gentle. You may feel more open, fragile and vulnerable than you are used to being. Take a shower or bath. Rest or sleep, if possible. It may be best to avoid socializing, as you have been to places few will understand or know how to support. Attempts to communicate your profound journey insights and experience to those who have never journeyed will likely fall on deaf ears. Avoid talking about your session with insensitive individuals who might make critical comments that breed doubts about the validity of your journey experience.

Give yourself sufficient time after your journey to assimilate and integrate the work you did. Jumping right back into your daily routine doesn't honor, or help facilitate, the deep healing process that's taking place. Allow yourself to just feel. Just be. If it was a difficult journey, make sure to pamper yourself.

Be aware of post-journey "contraction." During your journey, you may have experienced yourself in a hugely expanded state. After a big expansion, you'll likely contract--but not all the way back to who you were before the journey. Compared to the expanded version of yourself you experienced on your journey, it may not seem like you've changed in any way when you come down. Try not to prematurely evaluate your session. It may take a few days to notice results. For example, an ordinarily unemotional man feels powerful emotions on his journey. When he comes down, he's disappointed that he can no longer feel so intensely. A week later he realizes he is feeling emotions more deeply than he ever did before.

You might find it hard to sleep the night after your journey. You may need some sleep aids, like melatonin or Valium. Your dreams may be vivid that evening and over the next week. Or you may have no dreams at all.

If you have the ability to make a cocoon of your life for a couple days after your journey, you'll see better, faster results. Give yourself time to relax, recharge, and nurture your body, soul, and inner child. Get a massage. Reward yourself for all the courageous, difficult work you are doing. Set up an appointment with your sitter or therapist to help support, process, and integrate your journey experience. Give yourself time to assimilate and incorporate your experience into your psyche, body, and life. Follow up on any guidance received in your journey.

Sometimes intense emotions, moods, or physical symptoms that arise during a journey may persist for several days afterward. If major new material surfaced but was not fully processed, you may experience uncomfortable feelings and body sensations that could last until the next journey. For example, you might feel fragile, irritable, or sad. You might cry often. Physical symptoms might include stomach aches or other discomforts. Get support from a therapist, guide or bodyworker to help you process through this unfinished business.

Don't judge the session by what you think happened during the journey. Give it time to percolate. The real test of a journey's effectiveness will show up in the days and weeks afterward. Don't be disappointed if nothing dramatic happened during your journey. Gentle journeys can produce dramatic changes. Be alert for positive shifts in how you feel and how you react to things, people, and situations.

Psychedelic therapy greatly accelerates healing and transformation. As you continue journeywork, you might outgrow old friends and dysfunctional relationships. You may want to spend more time with kindred spirits who are healthy and inspiring.

15. USEFUL TECHNIQUES

Therapeutic techniques used in depth therapy can sometimes be applied to psychedelic work. With the aid of psychedelics, these techniques often work powerfully--even for those who have had no previous success with them. Here are some examples.

Inner Child Work

There are thousands of people who get up every morning giddy with wonder and excitement about the adventure of life. Most of them are under five years old!

Your inner child is the part of yourself that is feeling-oriented, soft, spontaneous, imaginative, innocent, and playful. The archetype of the child is often used as a symbol of the purity of the soul.

Most adults have grown distant from this vital part of themselves. To survive childhood trauma, this vulnerable part of yourself may have been secured within protective walls. MDMA is especially effective at melting these walls. When you first contact your inner child you may find that he or she is sad, angry, afraid, or distrustful. This wounded child needs to be seen, heard, felt, and loved in order for the adult self to heal. Your childhood is the foundation upon which your adult life is built. Until the foundation is repaired, everything you build upon it will be shaky.

In journeyspace, try reconnecting to your inner child by looking at photographs of yourself as a child. In an altered state, you may be able to see emotions in the child's eyes that tell you what he or she is feeling. Try dialoging with your child. Ask questions like: "What do you want to tell me?" "What do you need from me?" and "How can I make you feel better?" Wait and listen for answers. Trust the first response that comes to mind. Re-parent your child with comments like "I love you." "I will protect you." And "I will always be there for you." Praise your child with comments like "You are wonderful and lovable." Be a loving parent to your own inner child.

Provide toys, dolls, stuffed animals, and puppets to play with during journeys. Have crayons and a sketch pad to draw on. Allow yourself to draw and play. You may be surprised to discover how this can jog childhood memories, reveal unconscious material, and help work out childhood issues. It's never too late to have a happy childhood.

Caution: Reconnecting to your inner child is an important part of healing childhood wounds. However, prolonged regression to a childlike state can become a defense against more challenging shadow work. If you are being re-parented by your therapist, regression can become a way of staying dependent on the therapeutic relationship rather than growing into a responsible, strong adult.

Working with Photographs

In journeyspace, family pictures from childhood and photos of significant people in your past can stimulate insights, emotions, and memories. In an altered state you might detect body language, facial expressions, and family dynamics you never noticed before. Notice your positive or negative visceral and emotional reactions to each person in the photographs. If you have a strong response to someone, trust and explore your feelings.

Look at childhood photos of yourself at different ages. See if you can spot when you began to lose the brightness in your eyes. When did you start getting chubby or skinny? When did you start looking sad, scared, lost, or angry? These clues can jog memories and help construct a coherent story that verifies when trauma occurred.

Some photos may activate memories of long-forgotten kindness and support from caring people in your past that made you feel loved and important. Let these good feelings in!

If you have unfinished business with anyone in your photos, verbalize what you want to say to them.

Mirror Work

In journeyspace, looking at your face in a mirror can be powerful. Gazing gently into your eyes, ignore the rest of your face. Speak positive affirmations to yourself. Try saying "I love you." Dialog with yourself. Ask yourself important questions. This works especially well on MDMA.

WARNING: On LSD you may look hideous. Don't panic. It's just the drug!

Guided Meditations

A guided meditation at the beginning of a journey can help journeyers relax, move beyond thoughts, and get centered in their body. In a calming, hypnotic tone, a sitter might say something like this:

"Close your eyes and focus on the gentle rising and falling of your chest and belly with each breath. Rising and falling like gentle waves at the sea shore. Rising and falling. Rising and falling. Be aware of mother earth supporting your weight. Nothing to think about, nowhere you have to be, nothing you have to do. As you breathe, relax your toes, your feet, your calves, your thighs (keep directing attention to include the whole body). Breathe into any places in your body that feel tight, painful, or numb."

Guided meditations can occasionally be used to resource journeyers working through memories of traumatic events. For example, if the journeyer experiences being abused as a powerless child, a sitter can say something like, "Imagine you are no longer a powerless little child. Imagine you are a big, fearless adult or a fierce animal. What would you do and say to your abuser now? Imagine how it would feel to run away to the safety of a comforting relative or friend (real or imaginary)." This type of directed fantasy enables a journeyer to feel powerful where they once were powerless.

Guided meditations can also be used to reprogram childhood experiences of being abused or neglected by parents. A sitter can encourage the journeyer to imagine the feeling of having ideal parents, taking time to imagine scenarios of happy interactions with these caring parents. The journeyer can inhabit fantasies of being held and cherished by a warm, loving mother, or feeling safe and protected by a doting father.

For survivors of childhood sexual abuse, the sitter can suggest the journeyer imagine an ideal, first-time sexual scenario with a consenting peer. For those whose budding sexuality was shamed by adults, the sitter can suggest imagining growing up with adults who normalized and celebrated their emerging sexuality.

When guided meditations are used to reprogram traumatic events, they should never impose upon or interrupt the journeyer's unfolding process. They should never be used as a way to avoid the full impact and release of trauma. Use them as a resource to heal wounds that are already being felt and released.

When the rational, critical mind is bypassed in journeyspace, guided meditations with positive affirmations can sink deeply into the unconscious mind, reprograming traumatic memories and negative beliefs.

16. SUPPLEMENTAL PRACTICES THAT SUPPORT JOURNEYWORK

Bodywork

When stress is chronic or traumatic, our muscles respond with excessive or continuous contraction. If the trauma is too overwhelming to process, it's frozen and retained within the contraction. Muscles have memory, but not cognitive memory. They have memory like a pre-verbal child would have. Memory at this primitive level cannot be accessed by cognitive dialogue. Bodywork can directly access and release trauma at this non-verbal, often unconscious level.

MDMA deepens and accelerates bodywork. It lowers the pain threshold, allowing for more muscular release. It also enhances the journeyer's ability to engage at a feeling level.

A moderate dose of LSD can also enhance bodywork. It brings unconscious constriction and the emotional material locked inside into conscious awareness. The addition of MDMA or a low dose of psilocybin to LSD tends to promote releasing.

If you have training in a gentle form of bodywork, it can be successfully combined with therapeutic journeywork. When journeyers start feeling the effects of the medicine, or experience difficult passages during a session, their body tensions can increase.

When this happens, bodywork may be helpful. To keep the focus on psychological work, a full body massage is not recommended, but calming the body and relaxing tense muscles can reduce distractions. Touch can also speed healing by facilitating the release of old traumas that are held in the body.

Offer touch only if asked, or if it looks like it would be helpful, rather than a distraction from the journeyer's ongoing process. Touch is supportive only if you are truly comfortable touching the person in that moment. The body perceives much that's unspoken; reluctant touch can undermine the trust you've built with the journeyer.

"Holding" is the most underrated massage stroke, and often the best touch a person can receive. Holding is simply placing a hand gently on a specific spot with no movement. It can be unexpectedly difficult to do well. It requires allowing your hand to rest on another person without tension or movement. If you find tension entering your hand or arm, make sure you're in a completely comfortable position physically and mentally; breathe deeply and evenly. Then begin again.

When you touch the journeyer, patiently listen and watch for feedback. Proceed attentively. Listen for sounds and verbal messages as to how the touch is being received. For example, a long sigh is a sign of release and/or relaxation. Watch and feel for physical twitches or other movements. These can be signs of relaxation or of increasing tension. If you are not sure which, ask the journeyer: "How is this touch?" or "Is this working for you?"

It can be frustrating for a person to want a very specific kind of touch but not be able to explain it. Be willing to ask for feedback. Sometimes it's easiest to have the person demonstrate on your body exactly what they want. If they model their desired touch on your body, there are a number of factors to notice. Pay attention to where they touch and the amount of pressure they use. Notice what part of their hand they use and if they include another part of their body as well (maybe they lean against you as they hold). Notice whether their fingers are together or spread, whether their hand is flat or wrapped around the body part, whether they move the hand or hold it still. If they demonstrate fairly accurately, they will start feeling some sense of relief as if you were already touching them in that way.

The end of a session is an especially good time for bodywork. Use only gentle forms such as relaxing Swedish massage, energy work, craniosacral, or the Trager method.

Yoga

If you habitually live in your thoughts, you may have little awareness of your body's interior. Yoga promotes awareness of the inside of your body. You learn how breathing helps open up constricted places in your body. These constricted places may be holding in repressed feelings and memories that need to be reawakened, felt, and released in order to heal. A thorough practice of yoga will open these places and soften muscular armor that holds trauma. The more conscious you are of your inner body, the more productive your journeywork will be.

Note: Kundalini yoga is not the best type of yoga for promoting embodiment and the release of trauma. While it can affect the body in profound ways, it is specifically about consciously building and working with Kundalini energy that rises up the spine--connecting personal energy with the greater energy of Spirit. Rather than relaxing the muscles, it can increase the energy level in the body.

Meditation

Most of us are thinkers. Our culture stimulates, reveres, and rewards thinking. Thinking, however, is not productive for journeywork. The best work happens in places of no thought. If you are practiced at quieting your mind, you will be able to go deeper in journeyspace. Take time to cultivate a meditation practice. Turn off the internet and TV. Sit in silence. Breathe. Be fully present with yourself in the moment. Find your calm center within. If you make a habit of controlling the chatter in your head, it will be easier to get your mind out of the way when you journey.

Lifestyle

Psychedelic therapy will change your life--both inside and outside. If your outside life is too busy or structured to accommodate inner changes, you're better off postponing journeywork until more flexibility is available. High-intensity work or lifestyle demands are the antithesis of organic healing processes. To profit from journeywork, you need to devote time, energy, and attention to your inner life. You will need ample downtime for processing, self-care, and integration.

Allow for your life to change. You may be feeling things you have never felt before. You may experience new levels of consciousness that inspire you to change your habitual ways of being and living. The more rigid and unyielding your present life circumstances are, the harder it will be to allow a new you to come forth.

17. JOURNEY STORIES

PRENATAL MEMORIES

A fifty-year-old science teacher had worked through many issues in previous journeys with me, but still felt anxious and suicidal whenever he was alone. Many years of previous talk therapy hadn't helped. As he became adept at getting to the root of his feelings, he was able to identify the core fear: "When I'm alone I feel like I'm going to die."

During a journey using MDMA and LSD, he experiences being in a stark, white room full of bright light. He senses that he's in a hospital. It becomes clear that the bright lights are in a surgery room. He is there--in his Mother's belly.

"I see a knife coming towards me. It wants to kill me. Nowhere to escape. I'm very scared. I might die. I can't scream, yell, or talk. I'm totally helpless. Mother wants an abortion. That's why she came to the hospital. The doctor wants to put a knife in her vagina. At the last minute she got scared and said 'no.' I don't think the knife actually came inside."

All during this experience the journeyer's legs and body shake intensely. I ask him about the doctor: "I think he doesn't want to do the abortion. I sense he is very kind. I think he tries to convince Mom not to do it."

I ask him if there is anyone else in the room. "I see an image of a guardian angel. He wants to protect me. He has my good in mind. He protects me, I think, by not letting her do it--and making her change her mind." I ask the journeyer if the angel protected him later in life. He recounts six near-catastrophic incidents when his life was miraculously saved. In three of these cases, "something" told him to take quick action that prevented a serious accident.

A week after his journey, he reports that when he's alone he no longer feels like dying.

REGRESSION TO INFANCY

A businessman in his fifties struggled with depression, low self-esteem, and sex addiction. He was unable to love or connect emotionally with his wife and children. The following are excerpts from his first MDMA journey in which he spontaneously regressed to infancy.

"I'm a little baby. I'm in my crib, alone. I want someone to come spend time with me. My tummy hurts. I feel so empty." I (the sitter) give him a baby bottle filled with water. "My bottle is the only thing to fill my tummy. My bottle is all I have. I'm so alone. Mommy and Daddy are working. I cry for attention. That's the only way I can get someone to be there. They don't like me to cry.

"My nursemaid is all I have. She makes me feel like I am wanted. She takes care of me. I'd always look forward to her coming. I'd wait for her to come. I was alone and afraid. My body is shaking. All the pain I felt as a baby is coming up."

After the journey he reports:

"How absolutely real, authentic, and primal it was for me. While there, in the session, I'm connecting to my authentic self and the exiled parts of me are getting a chance to be expressed and seen by my adult self. I rediscovered my inner child. He was finally heard, and was able to talk about anything. I felt very open and vulnerable. I want this so much for myself. Simply, during the session, I can be real and risk letting all of those hurts, pains, shame, and memories that are sabotaging my adult life out into the light."

EMPOWERING THE MAJESTIC INNER PRIMATE

A journeyer recovering from childhood incest wrote this report of his empowering LSD session.

"I was barely a child when I was crushed under the weight of my father and older brother's shame and depravity. My power sucked from me before I even knew what power was. Later in life, I would develop all different kinds of counterfeit strengths that gave the impression that I was a man. But if you looked closely, you would have discovered an impersonator. A weak, damaged child wearing the skins of men--a TV director, a father, a coach, a teacher.

"Once I began a course of therapy using psychedelics in a controlled therapeutic setting there was no turning back. First I saw the crippled homunculus of that child trapped inside me. Then

I uncovered my childhood sexual abuse, shaking and thrashing uncontrollably as my body released the shame and pain put there by those who were supposed to protect me. Then, in my darkest place, a window opened that made me realize I was one of many who had been sexually abused as a child. A flood of compassion filled me. Then the shaking began again, but this time it was different. Something else was inside of me. Once I joined with it, strength and power flooded into me.

"Last week I had one of my most important journeys. Two hits of LSD manifested an ape-like primacy in me. I could feel its primal force, a beast fully born of the Earth, rising inside me. Grunting. Baring its teeth. Muscles rippling. I felt confident, dangerous, and--kind. I felt what it must have been like to have been a Neanderthal experiencing the gift of consciousness and wonder. My body, an animal full of power and grace, my heart and mind fixed on a wondrous eternity.

"Then I started to move, feeling the animal inside. I grabbed a wooden walking stick by the door and snapped it in half--showering the room in splinters. Gripping the two split halves, I felt like one of the apes in the "Dawn of Man" segment of Kubrick's 2001: A Space Odyssey. I started pounding the furniture, reveling in the discovery of this new power. Snarling in celebration. Becoming.

"It's important to know that this power is in fact a weapon. And like any weapon, it can be used to defend or attack. This power in the hands of my father was used to crush and humiliate. I was afraid of it. I was afraid of what it could do to people. The pain it could inflict. I wanted nothing to do with it. But this was not my power alone. This was something greater. As I felt it expand inside of me I experienced the humbling responsibility that comes with it. And I knew I wanted this. I knew I needed this, and I knew what my journey guide said was true: 'This power, full of compassion and understanding is what is needed right now if we have any hope to change the world.'

"I still have far to go but I feel eternally grateful for the teachers, teacher plants and other entheogens that have conspired to bring me out of my tomb of abuse and into the body of a man."

THE AUTHOR'S JOURNEY STORIES

In the initial phase of my psychedelic therapy, the medicines uncovered hard truths that I was an unwanted child who never had a warm, devoted mother to bond with. My father was distant, narcissistic, and mostly absent. I was raised by a series of paid nannies. I felt unloved and unsafe. The following narrative is from one of my early journeys.

HEALING MY INFANT TRAUMA

"An hour ago I ingested two hits of LSD. I am in a comfortable room with my trusted therapist. I close my eyes and begin to focus my attention into my body. I am surprised to discover that I feel sensations wherever I direct my awareness. Some places feel relaxed and tingly, some tight and jittery, some heavy, some numb. I can feel a whole universe inside my skin!

"My therapist directs me to scan my body to find places where there is pain. My belly feels constricted. There are pockets of sharp pain in my colon. I am asked to focus my attention and breathe into the pain. I struggle to quiet the incessant thoughts that distract attention away from my belly. I'm anxious. Deep breathing is difficult. I suddenly get very cold. My heart races, my teeth chatter, my body trembles. Even though I'm aware that I'm an adult participating in a psychedelic therapy session, I feel like an infant. I'm feeling terror from my childhood! My nursemaid is scary--she's hurting me. No one is protecting me. I feel alone and utterly helpless. Each time I breathe into the constrictions in my belly, my body releases more terror. I'm experiencing this nightmare as though it were happening right now.

"In the core of the tightness I feel Mommy doesn't want me, and nobody truly loves or cares about me. I burst into deep, gut-wrenching sobbing. It feels strangely purging. I weep, I wail, and with encouragement from my therapist, I scream and kick my legs. 'Stop! Get away from me! I hate you!' I'm amazed I've been carrying all this rage, fear, and sadness inside me all my life.

"For hours I continue to breathe into my belly. I'm immersed in powerful emotions and vivid memories of childhood. As I feel and release the trauma, the constriction and pain in my colon subsides. My therapist comforts my infant self, and I begin to feel a robust, new sense of well-being and peace.

"When the drug wears off, I am dumbfounded at the stark reality of events that happened to me forty years ago. How can a drug unlock these memories? How did I ever survive my childhood? No wonder I've been sick and depressed for so many years!"

HEALING MY SEXUAL ABUSE TRAUMA

As my parental wounds healed, new traumatic memories began to surface during an LSD/psilocybin session.

"'My lower back is frozen! It's so tight I can barely move.' My therapist helps me focus attention and breath into the tightness at the base of my spine. My pelvis feels numb. I'm nauseous and thirsty. I feel fear in my thighs and lower back. Everything is turning dark and scary. I'm breathing fast. My body is beginning to shake and spasm. I whimper like a child in a high-pitched voice. My legs start to run in place. My therapist asks me if the fear has words. I scream, 'I'm afraid, don't hurt me. STOP!' Suddenly, body memories of sexual abuse surface. There are no linear or visual memories, but my body is being jerked about like a limp rag doll. My body's intense, involuntary response is undeniable evidence that I am a little boy being anally raped. I sob, cough, and scream, 'Help me! I feel so helpless, unprotected, and unloved. He's threatening if I tell anyone, he'll hurt my mother.'

"I am immersed in this nightmare for hours. Finally, I feel the drug wear off and the cathartic releasing wind down. My therapist comforts me with a soothing belly rub. I gently sob. Tears flow. I don't want to believe I was raped. It's hard to accept this shocking revelation."

In subsequent sessions, I discovered and released rape trauma that was hidden in different places in my body. I felt layers of fear, pain, and anger that took dozens of journeys to work through. As I processed through the rape, sexual anxieties and dysfunctions I had lived with all my adult life began to vanish. Healing my sexual abuse transformed the myriad different ways the trauma had compromised my health and happiness.

As it turns out, my bleeding ulcers and depression were symptoms of deep, hidden wounds. Fixing my symptoms would have only addressed the tip of the iceberg. Looking back on my life, I appreciate how my symptoms were catalysts that pushed me onto a road less travelled.

Sometimes, life's challenges are dancing lessons from God.